CW01647326

Learn English

Improving Spoken English

Nicola Mee

Book 2

First published in 2018

Published by Sandford Press Limited

Hillside, Albion Street, Chipping Norton, Oxfordshire, OX7 5BH

ISBN 978-0-9957327-3-5

Author: Nicola Mee

Illustrator and designer: Lorraine Inglis

Printed and bound in the UK

Contents

Introduction: how to use this book

This book is for English students at B1/B2 level who want to improve their speaking and listening skills through self-study.

Each chapter is situation focused. You do not have to study every topic, but there are different language points in each chapter as well as vocabulary.

The course is designed to be used with a tablet or smart phone.

We recommend that you have:

- a good **English-English dictionary app** (**not** a translation app) to use for checking meaning grammar and most importantly **pronunciation** of new words. The Free Dictionary gives both British and American pronunciation, but there are many others.
- **a sounds app** for specific pronunciation work. **Sounds Pronunciation App** is free and you can type in the word and it will give you the pronunciation.
- a good **voice recognition app** e.g. Siri or Cortana, on iPhones and Windows Phones, or a good Android equivalent, to check your pronunciation.
- a means of **recording your voice and playing it back**, which you should be able to do on your mobile phone.

Using the book

The chapters all follow a structure designed to make it easy for you to learn English and guide you through the learning process.

Topic phrases: each chapter has several sections covering different aspects of the chapter content, and each section starts with sample phrases that you can use and adapt in similar situations. Key parts of the phrases are shown in black.

Podcast conversations: each chapter has four podcast conversations that you can download to your phone. The conversations put some of the sample phrases in context. As well as reading and understanding the conversations, it is important to listen to them on the podcasts and then practise speaking. Listen to, read and repeat the conversations as many times as you need to. Listen without the script the first time, then listen and read the second time (and third and fourth time if you need to). You will find all the podcasts for the chapters at www.learnenglish2.education.

Grammar: You will find grammar is explained at the end of each chapter. There is also a grammar guide at the end of the book. The explanations use the shorthand V1, V2, V3 and V-ing to describe the different verb forms as follows:

V1	V2	V3	V-ing
take	took	taken	taking
play	played	played	playing
go	went	gone	going

Key tips: important aspects of learning and using English are highlighted and explained.

Links to external content: for extra help some links are included to external content online.

Pronunciation: throughout the book you are encouraged to say key phrases to Siri/Cortana etc. on your phone. Does Siri understand? If it does, you are making good progress. There is also lots of advice to help you to get your intonation right.

Improve your vocabulary: each chapter has useful vocabulary for specific situations, and general language to help you in your speaking. Check new words using your dictionary app. Sometimes, try to understand generally without looking up every word. If you do this you will improve your listening skills more quickly. Your English-English dictionary is a good tool for learning new words, but you don't need to look up all the words to understand a conversation.

Learning new vocabulary

Language users have two kinds of vocabulary: **passive** (that we understand) and **active** (that we use). The method outlined below is designed to help you focus on improving your **active** vocabulary.

Each unit in the book contains many words, some of which you will be familiar with and some, you will be seeing for the first time. We suggest you consider which items of vocabulary will be most useful for you. We recommend that you select a small number of words/phrases, maybe five a week and **focus on activating** them using the method below. This doesn't mean you forget the other new vocabulary, but that you focus on **using** the words/phrases that you have chosen.

When you have chosen your items of vocabulary for the week:

1. Learn the correct pronunciation. Use online dictionary resources/ pronunciation apps for this.
2. Think about situations **in your life** when **you may use** this vocabulary. Write sentences using the language and memorise them.
3. Focus on using these sentences as often as possible in the week. Make sure you choose ones that you will be able to use.

Listening

To be good at speaking, you have to be good at listening. There are lots of things you can do to improve your listening skills in addition to listening to the podcast conversations:

- Watch films in English without subtitles. If you use subtitles you will improve your reading, but not listening skills. This may be difficult at first but gets much easier with regular practice.
- Listen to your favourite English music, first without, then with the words online.
- Listen to English language radio stations in the background while you are doing other things.
- Relax – you don't need to understand every word, and stress makes listening harder. Just keep calm, give yourself time and let your brain do the work.

Speaking

Speaking a language is like driving a car – you need to practise. With the aid of technology, this book enables you to practise your language before you try it out with other people. The aim of this book is to give you the structure to learn alone and really improve your fluency, pronunciation and confidence with speaking. Good luck, and remember, **practice makes perfect**!

Grammar items and grammar guide

You can find below items of grammar and question words that are used in specific situations in the various chapters in the book. Use these to help you learn key pieces of grammar and understand how they are used in situations.

Grammar

Grammar guide

1 At home

Talking about homes and family

Modern families are not as simple as mother, father, sisters and brothers. In lots of families there has been a divorce and a new marriage.

When parents aren't together you can say:

My parents are **separated**.
My mum and dad **split up**.
My folks are **divorced**./My parents got **divorced** [when]./My parents **divorced** [when].

When parents are in a new relationship you can say:

My dad's got a **new partner**.
My mum's **new boyfriend** came for dinner last week.
My dad met his **new wife** at work.

When parents are married to the new partner you can say:

My mum/dad **remarried** 3 years after the divorce.
I really like my **step-father/step-dad**.
My **step-mother/step-mum** is good for my dad.

When you have siblings (brothers and sisters) from a new relationship you can say:

(same mother different father or same father different mother)

My **half-sister** is just like our mum.
My **half-brother** looks like his dad.

(different parents, siblings from previous marriage)

My **<u>step</u>-brother** is 2 days younger than me.
My **step-sister** doesn't live with us, she stayed with her dad.

Look at Pilar's family tree and Abdulrahman's family tree.

Pilar's family tree

Pilar's mother, Laura, has three children; Carlos, Pilar and Ana. Ana is Carlos and Pilar's half-sister. Maria is Pilar's step-sister. Maria is Ana's half-sister. Carlos is Maria's step-brother.

Abdulrahman's family tree

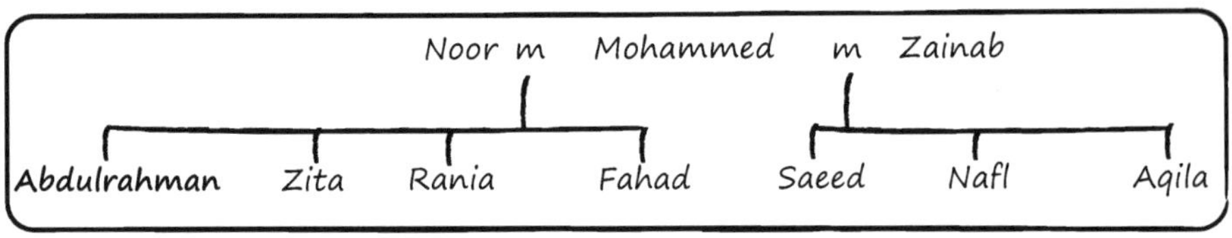

Saeed and Nafl are Abdulrahman's half-brothers, Aqila is his half-sister. Zainab is his step-mother.

Podcast conversation part 1

Abdulrahman: So, Pilar, what's your family like?

Pilar: It's a pretty normal Spanish family. My mum and dad are divorced. My mum remarried so I have a step-father, but my dad is single. What about you? Your family's huge isn't it?

Abdulrahman: Well, it's not considered huge in Saudi Arabia. My dad has two wives so I guess I have a kind of step-mum, and in total there are seven children: my mum has four – two sons and two daughters, and my step-mum has three – two boys and a girl, so I have one brother, two sisters and two half-brothers and a half-sister, but in my country they are just my brothers and sisters. What about you? Do you have many siblings?

Pilar: That sounds like a big family to me! I have an older brother, Carlos, and a younger half-sister, Ana. My step-dad, José, has a daughter, María, from his first marriage too so she's my step-sister.

Pronunciation

When native speakers speak English, they stress the important words, and the 'grammar' words (e.g. *does, do, from, for, an, the, than* etc.) become softer and sometimes difficult to hear.

Podcast for pronunciation

Listen to the difference between the three questions below.

1. What's María like?
2. What does María like?
3. What does María look like?

Repeat the questions and record yourself on your smartphone. Listen to your recording and compare with the podcast.

KEY TIP When speaking, people don't often say *mother* or *father*, this is very formal. They usually say *mum* and *dad*.

Describing people

To ask about someone's personality you can ask:

What's [name] **like?**

Grammar
See G1 on describing people on page 9.

You can answer:

He's/She's friendly.
Well, he's/she's really outgoing.
I'd say he's/she's quite confident.

Improve your vocabulary: *check new words using your dictionary app*

Positive	Neutral	Negative
intelligent	intellectual	geeky
determined	assertive/strong willed	bossy
gregarious/bubbly	outgoing	hyperactive
charming	nice	smarmy/creepy
self-assured	self-confident	arrogant
funny/witty	amusing	boring/dull
thoughtful	considerate	annoying/overbearing

For more personality adjectives go to: http://www.esolcourses.com/content/exercises/grammar/adjectives/personality/more-words-for-describing-personality.html

To give more information, you can add an adverb before the adjective.

0%					100%
not at all	a little a bit	quite (neutral) pretty (informal) rather (formal)	really	very	extremely incredibly unbelievably

You can say:

I find him rather **arrogant**.
Actually, he's not at all **bossy**.
I think she's pretty **intelligent**.
He comes across as quite **creepy**.
I'd say they're very **funny**.
I have to say I'm a little **strong-willed**.
We're incredibly **geeky**.

Podcast conversation part 2

Abdulrahman: What's your step-dad like?

Pilar: Well, it's interesting. He's *very* different from my dad who's *extremely* introverted and *quite* intellectual. I find Jose *pretty* outgoing and gregarious, and he has a *really* good sense of humour. What are your parents like?

Abdulrahman: I suppose I'd say my mum is *rather* shy and *a little* nervous around new people, but she's *really* kind and thoughtful. My step-mum is *a bit* younger than my mum so she's more like an older sister to me. She's *very* outgoing and *incredibly* witty.

Pilar: And what about your dad? What's he like?

Abdulrahman: My dad's older than both of them and he's *unbelievably* knowledgeable and charming, but *not at all* arrogant. They're a *pretty* good bunch.

Pilar: They sound it!

Pronunciation

Listen to the conversation between Pilar and Abdulrahman and focus on the words they stress. Practise reading both parts out loud and focus on the stress in each sentence.

Around town

Talking about places and buildings

To talk about places and buildings you can say:

In my opinion it's too congested.
I'd say it's quite vibrant.
Well, it's a sleepy town.
I suppose it's a bit overcrowded, but really cosmopolitan.

Improve your vocabulary: *check new words using your dictionary app*

Negative	Neutral		Positive
polluted	bustling	modern	picturesque
cramped	culturally diverse	historic	cosmopolitan
dirty	ancient	sprawling	compact
old fashioned	industrial	outdated	convenient
crumbling	commercial	touristy	lively
overcrowded	agricultural	old	vibrant
congested	suburban	sleepy	eco-friendly
claustrophobic	rural	peaceful	clean
run down	undeveloped	busy	scenic
dangerous	flat	hilly	safe

For more adjectives to describe places see:
http://www.slideshare.net/nuriamen/describing-places-32190635?next_slideshow=1

As with people, we can use **adverbs** to give more detail when describing places.
You can say:

I live in an **incredibly** beautiful area.
It's a **rather** congested city.
After dark it can be **quite** dangerous.
The city centre is **really** beautiful and has some extremely old buildings.

KEY TIP

1 Follow the word order **Adverb, Adjective, Noun**, e.g. 'It was an absolutely enormous house.'

2 Remember adjectives do not take the plural: '**big** houses', NOT '**bigs** houses'.

Grammar
See G2 on gradable and non-gradable adjectives on page 9.

Podcast conversation part 3

Abdulrahman: So, where do you live in Spain?

Pilar: I'm from Barakaldo, it's a city in the Basque Country, in the north of Spain.

Abdulrahman: Cool, what's it like?

Pilar: Well, it's pretty industrial but we have some really impressive scenery nearby. For example, we have an absolutely stunning coastline with great beaches for surfing or sunbathing, and we have some incredibly beautiful mountains for hiking or skiing in the winter. What about you?

Abdulrahman: I'm from Riyadh, the capital of Saudi Arabia. It's absolutely enormous, about 1,500km^2 and it's the commercial centre of my country. In my opinion, it's very congested as everyone drives a car. It isn't a touristy city, but there are some pretty interesting things to see.

Pilar: Oh, what would you recommend visiting?

Abdulrahman: Well, I'd say the Masmak Palace and the city gates are great if you like historical sites, and there are some very modern buildings that you should see too such as Kingdom Tower and the Burj Rafal, the tallest skyscraper in Saudi Arabia. What about Barakaldo?

Pilar: Well, it's right next to Bilbao so you have to visit the Guggenheim Museum which has some utterly amazing art exhibitions.

Pronunciation

Remember, when describing people or places, the verb ***be*** is weak (quieter) and we stress the descriptive words, e.g. 'Jane's a really nice girl.' Listen to Pilar and Abdulrahman, then practise reading their conversation.

Talking about your home

To talk about your home you can say:

I'm planning to buy **an apartment/a flat [us/uk]**.
In my country most people live in an **apartment building/a block of flats [us/uk]**.

I live in **a bungalow**.
Bungalow = single story house

I'm currently renting **a detached house**.
Detached = not attached to another house

I've just moved into **a semi-detached house**.
Semi-detached = attached to another house on one side

I used to live in **a terraced house**.
Terraced = attached on both sides to other houses in one building

I've always wanted to live in **a cottage**.
Cottage = smaller traditional home, often in the countryside

I own **a** two/three/four-**bedroomed** house/apartment.

KEY TIP

'Apartment' is used in American English and sometimes in British English. 'Flat' is only used in British English. And in Britain people often describe a house by how many bedrooms it has, rather than the number of square metres it is.

To give more information you can say:

It's got a big/small front/back garden.
There's a balcony.
I want to build a patio/deck area.
My bedroom has an en-suite shower room.
For me, a garage **is essential.**
We've just put in a wetroom.
We spend most of our time in the kitchen-diner.
My house has a lovely open-plan living area.
I need a bigger garden shed.

Podcast conversation part 4

Pilar: So with such a big family, you must have a big house? Do you all live together?

Abdulrahman: I suppose houses in Riyadh are generally quite big. We have a detached house, which has two apartments and a family area. My mum has the ground floor for us and my step-mum lives in the apartment upstairs with her children. Dad divides his time between both apartments, but we spend a lot of time together as one big family. We have a really big garden which goes all around the house and a large garage for the cars. What about you?

Pilar: Well, it's very different in Barakaldo. Most people in my city live in large blocks of flats. Most flats have a small balcony and an underground parking space. In our flat we've got an open-plan kitchen diner and a separate lounge. We've got three bedrooms, one has a small en-suite wetroom and then we have the family bathroom.

Time to Talk

1. Listen to all four parts of the podcast conversation between Abdulrahman and Pilar, which you will find at www.learnenglish2.education. Notice the weak forms when they are speaking. Then practise reading the dialogues. Record yourself on your phone then listen back. Do you sound like the speakers? Keep practising until you get it right.

2. Practise speaking about your own family and home using the vocabulary above. Use Siri/Cortana/voice recognition software to check your pronunciation. If the voice recognition software can understand you, you are doing well!

Remember, the more you practise, the better you will be.

Grammar

G1 Describing people

What's... like? is used to ask about someone's personality, e.g.:

What's Ana like? *She's friendly and outgoing.'*

What does... like? is used to ask about someone's likes and dislikes, e.g.:

What does Carlos like? *He likes football.*

What does... look like? is used to ask about appearance, e.g.:

What does Saeed look like? *He's tall and slim.*

G2 Gradable and non-gradable adjectives

Adjectives can be **gradable** and **non-gradable**.

Gradable means they can be a little bit or a lot, e g. happy – you can be a little happy or very happy. Other gradable adjectives are:

busy
crowded
positive
sweet
considerate
nice
fun
old
popular

Non-gradable adjectives can be one of three types: **extreme**, **absolute**, or **classifying** and they can't be modified using the adverbs on p. 5.

- **Absolute**, e.g. alive – you are alive or you are not alive, you can't be a bit alive.
- **Extreme**, e.g. terrified – if you are very frightened, you are terrified.
- **Classifying**, e.g. chemical – 'There's a chemical factory in my city' – that's the kind of factory it is.

Absolute adjectives can be used with these adverbs: **absolutely**, **virtually**, **totally**.

Extreme adjectives can be used with these adverbs: **absolutely**, **utterly**, **extremely**, **really**.

Classifying adjectives can be used with these adverbs: **essentially**, **mainly**.

The table below gives some examples:

Non-gradable	Type of non-gradable
dead/alive married/divorced/single unique	absolute
enormous/tiny filthy/spotless awful/excellent	extreme
indoor English financial	classifying

2 Socialising

Inviting people to do something...

To invite someone to do something you can ask:

Would you like to go for a coffee?
Do you want to grab some lunch?
Do you fancy going to the cinema with me?
How about we head to the beach?
I'm going to the pub on Saturday **if you'd like to join me.**
Why don't we go for a drink on Saturday?

> **! KEY TIP**
>
> In English, 'go for a drink' usually means alcoholic drinks, often in the evening; 'go for coffee' means non-alcoholic drinks in the daytime. When people say 'we must have a coffee', this isn't an actual invitation. You should **never** say no to this kind of invitation.

To make casual invitations without giving a specific time, you can say:

We should go for a drink.
We ought to get together more often!
We must catch up soon.

To reply to this kind of invitation, you can say:

Definitely!
Yeah, that'd be great!
Absolutely!
Let's do that.
Yes we must!

Grammar
See G3 on verb forms in phrases on page 19.

Podcast conversation part 1

In the street

Hannah:	Hi, Alberto! How are you? It's been ages!
Alberto:	Oh my God Hannah! Hi! How are you? Wow. Yeah, it must be, what, 5 years?
Hannah:	Yeah, something like that. Time flies hey? So, what are you up to these days?
Alberto:	Oh you know, busy busy busy. Listen, I'm really sorry I can't stop to chat but do you fancy meeting up at the weekend?
Hannah:	Sounds great. Are you still on the same number?
Alberto:	Yeah, call me and we'll arrange dinner on Saturday.
Hannah:	Great, look forward to it.

On the phone

Alberto:	Hello.
Hannah:	Hi Alberto, it's Hannah, I'm just calling about Saturday.
Alberto:	Hi, I'm so glad you called, so would you like to come over for dinner?
Hannah:	Are you sure? I don't want to put you to any trouble.
Alberto:	It's no trouble, I love cooking.
Hannah:	Then that sounds great. Do you want me to bring dessert?
Alberto:	OK, deal. I'll text you my new address.
Hannah:	Excellent. So I'll see you at say seven?
Alberto:	Seven's perfect, see you then.

Pronuncation

When we speak fluently in English as we saw in Chapter 1, words often melt together, so 'Do you' becomes /**dʒuː**/ and similarly with would you which becomes /**wʊdʒuː**/

Podcast for pronuncation

Listen to the podcast and repeat the questions:

1 Do you fancy...
2 Would you like to...
3 Do you want to ...

KEY TIP **Showing interest**

Part of having a natural conversation is reacting to what someone is saying and showing interest. This tells the speaker we understand and we want them to continue speaking. It can be hard to remember to give this feedback when you are trying to understand the language, but it is a very important part of fluent, effective communication.

When speaking English, you should use your facial expressions to communicate. We do this without thinking in our native language, but often when we are listening to another language we use a 'concentrating' face which makes it difficult for the speaker to understand how we feel.

Next time you speak in English, focus on using the vocabulary below and your facial expressions to communicate to the other person that you are listening and understand what they are saying.

Improve your vocabulary: check new words using your dictionary app

Positive	Neutral	Negative
Wow!/Cool! That's amazing! Great!/Fantastic! How interesting. I'm so happy for you.	Mmhmm/Uh huh OK/Yeah Oh right Really? I don't believe it.	Oh no!/That's a shame. I'm so sorry. That's awful! Poor you. How horrible!

Pronunciation

These phrases should not interrupt a story, but encourage the speaker to continue. Listen to how you use phrases like this in your own language. In English people usually say them in a slightly quieter voice than the person speaking. Remember to use facial expressions too.

Podcast conversation part 2

Saturday night at Alberto's house

Alberto: So what have you been doing since I last saw you?

Hannah: Well, I got a new job in London [Mmmmm] so I moved there and got a lovely apartment, but I really didn't enjoy the job [that's a shame] so I decided to take some time off and go travelling.

Alberto: Wow. So where did you go?

Hannah: Well, I decided to do some things I've always wanted to do [yeah] so first I went to Tonga and swam with humpback whales.

Alberto: Oh my God, that's amazing!

Hannah: Yeah, it was, and after that I went to New Zealand for a couple of days to catch up with my cousin, [right] but that wasn't such a good idea because I was mugged [Oh no] yeah, and they took my passport [that's awful], so I had to wait for a week there while I got a replacement sorted, and then I went to Fiji [uh huh] and dived with bull sharks [Wow!] and spent a couple of weeks just chilling on the beach.

Alberto: Cool! It sounds like you had an amazing time. I've always wanted to go to the South Pacific.

Pronunciation

Listen to the conversation and read the phrases. Then read it aloud first being Hannah, then try Alberto's part and record yourself on your smartphone. Listen to your recording and compare with the podcast. Repeat this until you are happy with your pronunciation.

Saying 'no' to an invitation...

To say 'no' to an invitation you can say:

I'm sorry but the tenth **isn't possible.** *(formal)*
I'm sorry I won't be able to make it.
I'm afraid I can't make next Thursday.
I'm sorry, I can't do the 25th.
I'm afraid 6 o'clock's not good for me.
Saturday**'s not gonna happen.** *(informal)*

! KEY TIP Remember when we are saying 'no' it is polite to start with 'I'm afraid' or 'I'm sorry'.

To rearrange for a different time or date you can ask:

Would it be possible to change the date?
Do you think we could postpone until July?
I'm already booked for Friday night, **can we make it** Saturday?
Let's do it another time; how about next Wednesday?
Can we take a rain check?

Rain check = rearrange for a later date

It is polite to explain why you can't go. You can say:

I have a prior engagement.	=	*I have already agreed to do something else.*
I've got so much on at the moment.	=	*I have a lot of things to do.*
I'm double booked.	=	*I have another thing to do at that time.*
I'm tied up with/doing...	=	*I'm busy doing something else.*
I'm in the middle of...	=	*I'm doing something which I haven't finished and I need to do.*
I'm snowed under at work.	=	*I have a lot of work to do.*

Pronunciation

To practise saying 'yes' and 'no' to invitations, record your voice on your phone asking to do something, then practise responding to the invitations. Here are some invitations you can use for practise:

Do you fancy going for a coffee this afternoon?

Would you like to come to the cinema with me on Tuesday?

Do you want to go for pizza on Saturday?

Make sure you speak out loud. Just reading and deciding your answer won't help improve your speaking.

Checking information...

When you're not sure you heard a detail correctly you can ask:

Am I hearing this correctly; you want to go to an Italian restaurant?
Sorry did you say Monday?
Was that 4th April?
Do you mean this one?

Are you saying you want me to help?
Can I just check, did you say 8 o'clock?
So let me get this straight, you're saying that you don't want to come?
Hang on, did I hear that right; they didn't call or let you know?

Grammar
See G4 on questions for checking information on page 19.

Podcast conversation part 3

Hannah: Thank you so much for dinner, it was lovely. I never knew you were such a great cook. You must let me return the favour.

Alberto: That'd be lovely. Just tell me when and I'll be there.

Hannah: Excellent, I'll call you.

On the phone

Alberto: Hi Hannah, how are you?

Hannah: Hi, I'm fine, thanks. Listen, I was just calling to see when you can come over for dinner. I'm free this weekend if that's any good for you?

Alberto: Did you say this weekend?

Hannah: Yes, I was thinking Saturday if that's any good for you?

Alberto: That would have been lovely, but I'm afraid I can't. I'm already double booked on Saturday.

Hannah: No worries, what about Sunday?

Alberto: Again, I'd love to but I'm in the middle of rehearsals for the concert next month and I'm tied up with that all weekend. [uh huh] Can we take a rain check until I'm not so snowed under with work, the kids and orchestra?

Hannah: Sure. I know how you feel. I've got so much on at the moment sometimes I just want to run away and go travelling again!

Alberto: Haha, let's go together! OK, how does 4th April suit you for dinner? I'm just looking in my diary and it looks like I'm free that weekend.

Hannah: Just a sec, let me check... Sorry, was that 4th April?

Alberto:	Yes,
Hannah:	Ugh, that's no good for me, although I could do lunch instead of dinner?
Alberto:	Perfect, let's do that.

Pronunciation

Listen to the conversation and focus on the pronunciation. Then read it aloud, first take Hannah's part, then try Alberto's part and record yourself on your smartphone. Listen to your recording and compare it with the podcast. Repeat this until you are happy with your pronunciation.

Making small talk...

Small talk is casual conversation in a social situation. The topics are unimportant matters.

To introduce a small talk topic, you can say:

So, what's new?
Have you been following the football?
Did you hear about that kid in Australia?
Did you see the newspaper this morning?
How's work **going?**
Speaking of changes, have you heard about the new road they want to build in town?
So, how are you getting on with the house renovations?
What's been happening in your world recently?
Any news on the promotion?
What do you think about this crazy summer we're having?

Typical small talk topics include:

At a party (with strangers)	At work	With friends
the weather TV programmes/films sporting events national events music	public transport the weekend traffic local town matters the company	food/exercise DIY/home maintenance family/pets celebrity news/pop culture social media – Facebook etc.

Podcast conversation part 4

Lunch at Hannah's house

Hannah: So glad you could make it. I wasn't sure when it started to snow yesterday! It's crazy, snow. In England. In April!

Alberto: Speaking of snow, did you hear about the lady that got stuck in her car for 6 hours?

Hannah: I know; awful! The town comes to a complete standstill every time it snows.

Alberto: I really wish they'd invest some money in gritting the roads and snow ploughs so that life can continue when we have a little bit of snow!

Hannah: I agree, it's ridiculous. In my town in France when it snows the council clears the roads and we carry on. I bet it's even better in Norway?

Alberto: Yeah, I mean, we don't get too much snow in Oslo, but up in the north life goes on when it snows. Although I suppose in England we just don't have enough snow to justify spending money on snow ploughs as it only snows for 4 days a year.

Hannah: I suppose so. Hey did you see *EastEnders* last night?

Alberto: No, I missed it. I was upstairs with Matteo helping him to finish painting the new bathroom.

Hannah: Of course. How's that going?

Alberto: We've almost finished now. Just the shower to do and it'll be ready for when mum visits next week.

Hannah: Sorry, did you say this week?

Alberto: No, she's arriving on Friday next week.

Hannah: Great!

Time to Talk

1. Listen to all four parts of the podcast conversation between Alberto and Hannah at www.learnenglish2.education. Notice their pronunciation then practise reading the dialogues. Record yourself on your phone then listen back. Do you sound like the speakers?
2. Use Siri/Cortana/voice recognition software to check your pronunciation of the vocabulary. If the voice recognition software can understand you, you are doing well!

Remember, the more you practise, the better you will be.

Grammar

G3 Verb forms in phrases for inviting people to do something

Offer	Activity	Time phrase
Would you like to	(+ V1) go for a drink	on Saturday evening?
Do you want to	(+V1) head to the cinema	at the weekend?
Do you fancy	(+V-ing) having dinner with me	tomorrow?
How about we	(+V1) see that new film	one day next week?
We should	(+V1) get together	soon.
We ought to	(+V1) go for coffee	some time.
You must	(+V1) come over for dinner	one day.

G4 Questions for checking information

Checking phrase	Information	Example
Am I hearing this correctly;	+ positive or negative phrase (NOT interrogative form)	• Am I hearing this correctly; you don't want chocolate cake? • Am I hearing this correctly; he stole your car?
Sorry, did you say	+ positive or negative phrase	• Sorry, did you say there is coffee? • Sorry, did you say you can't come?
Was that	+ noun phrase	• Was that ten o'clock?
Do you mean	+ positive or negative phrase + noun phrase	• Do you mean turn it off completely? • Do you mean he hasn't finished the project? • Do you mean 8 a.m. or 8 p.m.?
Are you saying	+ positive or negative phrase	• Are you saying that it's too expensive? • Are you saying it won't be big enough?
Can I just check, did you say	+ positive or negative phrase	• Can I just check, did you say it starts at 6.30? • Can I just check, did you say there aren't any tickets?

So let me get this straight,	+ positive or negative phrase (NOT interrogative form)	• So let me get this straight, (you're saying) Jim loves Abi? • So let me get this straight, they aren't leaving until June?
Hang on, did I hear that right?	+ positive or negative phrase + interrogative form	• Hang on, did I hear that right; they're building a new house? • Hang on, did I hear that right; she isn't pregnant? • Hang on, did I hear that right; has he got a new job?

3 People and relationships

Talking about love

Relationships have many stages.

When someone is attracted to another person you can say:

I fancy Lei from Accounting.
Sarah**'s got a crush on** Pierre.
Elaine**'s got a thing for** Dave.
I really like that guy.
My brother's **interested in** the girl from the coffee shop.
Tom**'s got the hots for** Alex.

If you are at the beginning of a relationship you can say:

It's casual at the moment.
I'm dating Jenny.
I'm going out with Maria.
I'm seeing someone. We've been out a couple of times.

When you are in an established relationship you can say:

It's serious.
I'm in a relationship with somebody.
I'm with Alberto.
We live together.

When you talk about marriage you can say:

I proposed to Hazel and she said yes!
We're engaged/I'm engaged to somebody; we'll probably get married next year.
They're going to tie the knot; I can't believe they're actually getting married!
We're getting married next year.
I'm going to marry him.

Improve your vocabulary: *check new words using your dictionary app*

To describe **your partner and members of their family** you can use the following:

boyfriend/girlfriend
partner
fiancé/fiancée
husband/wife
mother-in-law/father-in-law
sister-in-law/brother-in-law

Podcast conversation part 1

Paolo: Phil, I'm so glad you could come.

Phil: No worries, it's been a while. How've you been?

Paolo: Fine, and you?

Phil: Yeah, good thanks mate. So, what brings you here today?

Paolo: Well, the reason I called is because of a woman.

Phil: Paolo, with you it's always a woman! Last time I saw you, you were seeing another new girl, weren't you?

Paolo: Hahaha, Phil, I was dating five girls when I last saw you, but they were just casual, nothing serious.

Phil: And now?

Paolo: Well, interesting you ask. That's why I'm here in Australia. I met a wonderful girl back in Bologna, and at first we thought we couldn't be together because long distance relationships never work out, but then my job brought me here to Sydney and things got serious.

Phil: Wow, that's great! You say serious, how serious?

Paolo: That's the reason I called you actually. I'm planning to propose to her tonight.

Phil: Congratulations mate, that's awesome! I don't suppose you can tell me how you're going do it?

Paolo:	Absolutely! In fact, I need your help.
Phil:	Sure, just let me know what I can do.
Paolo:	I want to do it on the steps of the Opera House at sunset, and I need somebody to arrange the picnic with candles and champagne while I get Cristina.
Phil:	That's a good plan. I'm in.

Pronunciation

When we ask questions in English, our voice usually goes up at the end of the sentence, whereas when we are making a statement, our voice goes down at the end to indicate we have finished that piece of information. Listen and compare the pronunciation of the language below in the podcast for pronunciation.

Podcast for pronunciation

Do you fancy going to the cinema?

I'd like to go to the cinema.

Anything else?

No, that's it thanks.

Are you still on the same number?

I'm on the same number.

Grammar

See G5 on asking questions in English on page 29.

Getting married

Improve your vocabulary: *check new words using your dictionary app*

To talk about **weddings** you can use the following:	
hen do/night [UK/Australia]	honeymoon
bachelorette party [US]	bride
stag do/night [UK]	groom
bucks party [Aus]	maid of honour *(not married)*
bachelor party [US]	matron of honour *(married)*
wedding	best man
ceremony	bridesmaid
wedding breakfast	ushers
reception	wedding party
wedding list	spouse

! KEY TIP You get married **to** somebody NOT **with** somebody.

Podcast conversation part 2

Phil: Paolo buddy, I can't believe you're finally engaged!

Paolo: I know! For a second I thought she was going to say 'no', but then she smiled and it was OK! Now I suppose I need to start thinking about the wedding.

Phil: Yeah, planning a wedding is a nightmare, especially when all the families want to get involved. I suppose Cristina will do most of the planning, won't she?

Paolo: Well, yes, she will plan the wedding in Australia, but we must also have a small celebration in Italy after for my friends and family, so I will have to help her plan that with my Mother. Listen, I wanted to ask you, for the Australian wedding, I'd like to know if you would be my best man?

Phil: Wow, of course! Does that mean I get to plan the bucks party?

Paolo: Yes. Of course!

Phil: Cool. So when's the wedding?

Paolo: Cri wants to get married on the beach so we're thinking about February. She's looking for invitations and when she finds some she likes we will send them to everybody.

Phil: Great, so we have 4 months to plan.

Paolo: Well, we don't have to do much; Cri's choosing the colours, and flowers. We have to get the cake and rings, and the bridal party will be her family and you, so to be honest I don't have too much to worry about.

Phil: I meant the bucks party!

Paolo: Hahaha.

Pronunciation

Listen to the podcast conversation and read the phrases. Then read it aloud and record yourself on your smartphone. Listen to your recording and compare with the podcast. Repeat this until you are happy with your pronunciation.

When things go wrong in a relationship

To talk about problems in your relationship you can say:

We're going through/we've hit **a rocky/rough patch.**
Things are difficult in the relationship at the moment.

Things aren't so good at home.
When you live together and are having problems in your relationship.

We're having a **trial separation**.
To see if we want to break up permanently

We're **taking some time apart**.
We haven't completely broken up but we're not spending time together.

We've **broken up/split up**.
The relationship has finished.

We're **going our separate ways**.
We're not staying together.

We're **getting a divorce/getting divorced**.
We're ending our marriage.

To explain to other people why a relationship has ended you can say:

We **wanted different things.**
We wanted to pursue different interests or way of living.

It didn't work out.
The relationship ended.

We grew apart.
Both people changed and weren't good together any more.

He/She **cheated on** me.
My partner had a relationship with another person while they were with me.

He/She **had an affair.**
My partner had a relationship with another person while they were with me.

He had a mistress.
A married man's lover is called a 'mistress'.

She had a lover.
A married woman's extra-marital partner is called a 'lover'.

To explain what will happen after a relationship breaks up you can say:

We're going **to stay friends.**
We will see each other afterwards as friends.

It's all **amicable.**
We both agree and it is a friendly break-up.

To break up with somebody you can say:

I'm sorry, but **I don't think we should see each other anymore.**
I'm sorry, but **I don't think we have a future.**
I'm sorry, but **it's just not working for me.**
I think we want different things.
It's not you, it's me.
I just need some time for myself right now.
I just don't have time for a relationship at the moment.

Life after marriage

When a marriage ends you can say:

I'm divorced.
I'm a divorcee.

We have **joint custody of** the kids.
We share the responsibility for the children.

I have sole custody of the kids.
I have legal responsibility for the children.

I pay alimony/maintenance [us/uk].
I give money to my ex-partner.

I pay child support.
I give money to my ex-partner to support my children.

When your husband or wife has died you can say:

I'm a widow.
If you are a woman.

I'm a widower.
If you are a man.

Podcast conversation part 3

Paolo: So, Phil, what about you? You used to be married didn't you?

Phil: I did. A long time ago. I've been divorced for 9 years.

Paolo: Do you mind telling me what happened?

Phil: Oh the usual story. We married too young, didn't think it through. She wanted one thing, I wanted another.

Paolo: Oh really? That's so sad.

Phil: Ah, it is what it is – I like to put it down to experience. She's a great girl and we're friends now, but for a while there we were at each other's throats all the time.

Paolo: Why?

Phil: Well, I was away working all the time; mostly in Italy actually, and she was lonely.

Paolo: Yes, I remember you were in Bologna for a long time.

Phil: Yeah, well, she ended up having an affair with a colleague at her work. I came home and found out. We had a big fight, yelled and blamed each other, then she told me she wasn't happy and asked for a divorce.

Paolo: What did you say?

Phil: What could I say? I was really angry at first, then we sat down and talked it through and realised we were better as friends, so we got a divorce and for the last 8 years we've been friends.

Paolo: It's nice that you can still be friends.

Phil: Yeah, well, we were only married for 2 years and neither of us earned very much money in that time and we didn't have any kids so we didn't have things like alimony or child support to fight about. I think that made it easier.

Talking about disagreements

To talk about disagreements you can say:

Mild/calm	Medium/annoyed	Strong/angry
We had a disagreement. We had a bit of a discussion.	We had an argument.	We had a (big) fight. We had a row. We quarrelled.

To describe a couple who can't agree you can say:

They're **at loggerheads.**
They cannot and will not agree.

They're **at each other's throats.**
They are attacking each other verbally a lot.

They've **reached a stalemate.**
Neither of the people in the relationship will change their view.

Podcast conversation part 4

Phil: Congratulations mate, you survived the wedding!

Paolo: Well, in Australia, we still have the Italian version to go… and Mamma and Cri have been at loggerheads all week about flowers!

Phil: They'll get over it. People always argue about weddings; especially with the in-laws!

Paolo: Well, I for one can't wait for the honeymoon when all the rows will be over and we can just be happy!

Phil: I'll drink to that! Cheers!

Paolo: Cheers!

Time to Talk

1. Listen to all four parts of the podcast conversation between Phil and Paolo at www.learnenglish2.education. Notice their pronunciation, then practise reading the dialogues. Record yourself on your phone then listen back. Do you sound like the speakers?
2. Use Siri/Cortana/voice recognition software to check your pronunciation of the vocabulary. If the voice recognition software can understand you, you are doing well!

Remember, the more you practise, the better you will be.

Grammar

G5 Asking questions in English

You can ask questions in several different ways in English:

- **Direct questions:** where you ask the person directly for the information.
- **Question tags:** where you state the information and ask the person for confirmation.
- **Indirect questions:** where you ask if the person would mind giving you some information – usually used in formal situations, but also when you are unsure if you will get a reply *(see Chapter 5 for more information)*.

Direct questions

These are the most common types of questions and they can be closed or open:

Closed questions (only 'yes' or 'no' answers)

Do you like pizza?
Are you married?
Have you seen the new Bond film?

Open (many possible answers)

What kinds of food do you like?
Where did you get married?
What did you think of the new Bond film?

(For more information on word order in questions, see the ***Grammar guide*** *on page 126.)*

Question tags

Question tags are used more to confirm information we think we know, but are not completely sure about.

Affirmative statement +	**negative question tag**
You'*ve* been to Paris,	*haven't* you?
James works for the UN,	*doesn't* he?
Sophie *can* play the piano,	*can't* she?

Negative statement +	**affirmative question tag**
Toby *won't* come to the party,	*will* he?
Mohammed *isn't* taking that exam,	*is* he?
She *had* never flown before,	*had* she?

Notice how the *auxiliary verb* in the question tag matches that in the statement.

Look at podcast conversation 1 to see how each type of question is used between the friends.

4 Talking about health and lifestyle

Conditions and illnesses

It can be difficult to talk about people with illnesses or disabilities, and more so if you don't have the right words and expressions.

You can say:

A person who has + noun
A person who is + adjective
A person with + condition

He's/She's + adjective, e.g. 'Trevor's deaf.'
He/She suffers from + condition, e.g. 'He suffers from eczema.'
He's/She's got + condition, e.g. 'She's got learning difficulties.'

! KEY TIP 'Suffers from' is only used for conditions or diseases and not for a disability.

When somebody doesn't come to work because of illness you can say:

Khaled's **off sick.**
He is not coming to work because of illness.

My boss has been **signed off** for a month with stress.
The doctor says he/she cannot work.

India's **got a doctor's note.**
A doctor's note is a letter from the doctor to say that someone can't work due to illness.

Ed's **taking a personal day. [US]**
He's not coming to work for personal reasons.

Dan's **pulling a sickie. [UK]**
He's telling work he is ill when he isn't.

Sze's **having a duvet day.**
She's staying at home relaxing.

I'm **feeling pretty rough** today.
I'm feeling quite ill.

Pat's been **under the weather** for a week or so now.
She's been feeling ill.

Podcast conversation part 1

Amanda: Tris, do you know why Reiss hasn't been at work this week?

Tris: I think he's been signed off sick.

Amanda: Oh really? What's wrong with him? I've noticed he's been acting a bit strangely for a little while now. On Friday he walked out in the middle of the meeting. You know, he hasn't been himself, is he OK?

Tris: To be honest, I'm not sure. I know he suffers with his health and has a lot of problems with his stomach. I think he said he had IBS but they were still doing tests; it might be something to do with that.

Amanda: Well, whatever it is, I hope he feels better soon; I can't do all this on my own!

Tris: No, we don't want you signed off with stress as well as Reiss being off!

More detailed parts of the body

Improve your vocabulary

To discuss your health you need to know the words for parts of the body. Take a look at the diagrams below.

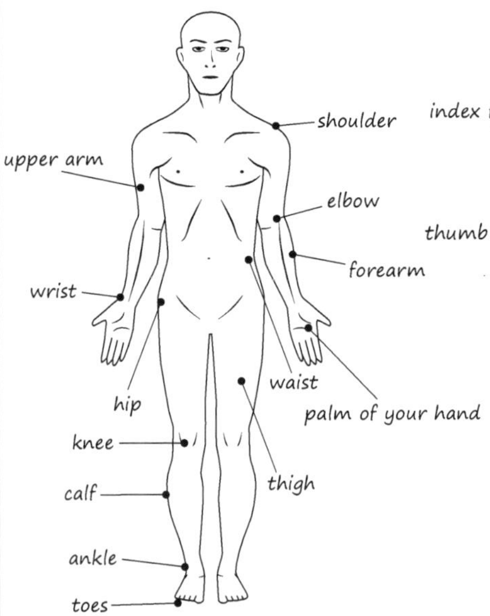

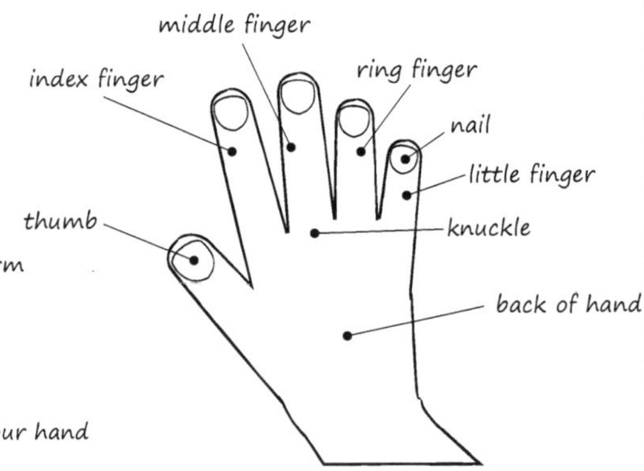

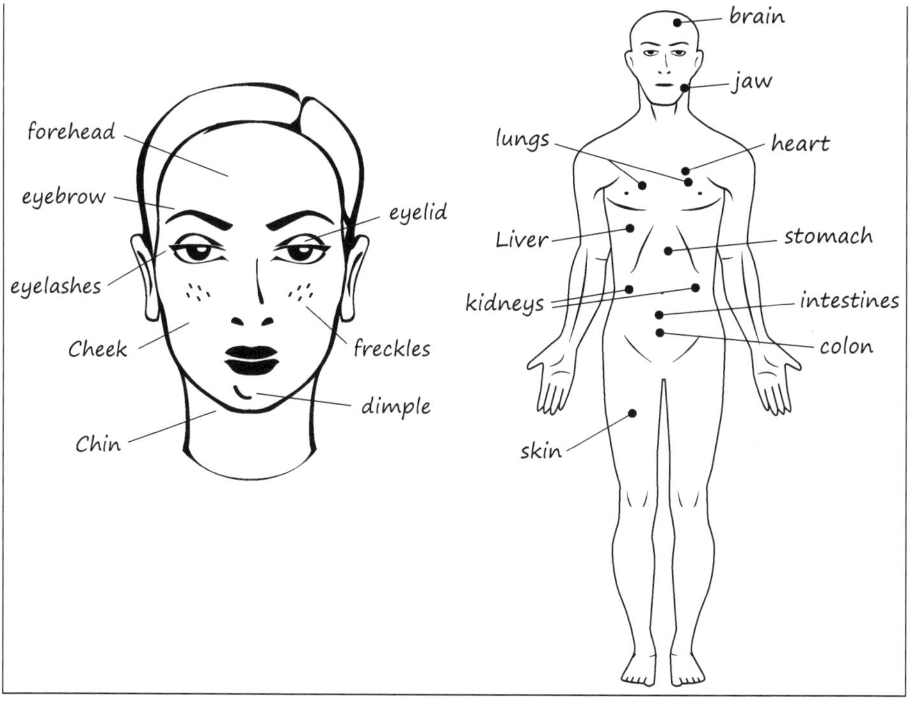

Pronunciation

To check how to say any new words such as those listed in 'Improve your vocabulary', type them into your pronunciation app and listen and repeat. Focus on the stress and note any silent letters. Repeat the word, record yourself and compare to the app.

Medical procedures

If you have to go to hospital for a procedure you can say:

I've **got an out-patients appointment.**
I'm going to hospital but just for the day.

He's/She's **been admitted to hospital.**
She/he will stay in hospital overnight.

He's/She's going under the knife.
He's/She's having surgery.

I've got to go in for a check-up.
I've got to have an MRI.
They want to do some tests. **[UK]**
They want to run some tests. **[USA]**
I need an operation to replace my hip joint.
I have to have surgery on my knee.
They're booking me in for a gastric bypass.
I'm on the waiting list for a kidney transplant.
I'm hoping to have my tonsils out.

Podcast conversation part 2

Amanda: Tris, I called Reiss last night.

Tris: Oh right? How is he?

Amanda: Unfortunately he's not great. He went to hospital yesterday and he was admitted.

Tris: Why? What happened?

Amanda: Well, he's been feeling ill for the past few weeks and at first the doctor thought it might be IBS because of his symptoms.

Tris: Right, that's what I thought he said.

Amanda: But he got a lot worse over the weekend and had to call an ambulance. They got him to hospital and the doctors did some initial tests, you know, blood tests, MRI, to try to find out what was wrong.

Tris: And?

Amanda: It turns out they think he has a tumour in his stomach. They were doing tests when I spoke to him. They should have the results today.

Tris: That's awful! Can we go and see him?

Amanda: Well, he said no visitors today but maybe tomorrow.

Tris: OK, well I can drive us after work if you like?

Amanda: Great, thanks.

Pronunciation

Listen to the conversation and read the script. Then read both Tris and Amanda's parts aloud and record yourself on your smartphone. Listen to your recording and compare with the podcast. Repeat this until you are happy with your pronunciation.

Grammar

See G6 on past tenses on page 40.

Diet and lifestyle

To talk about how active you are you can say:

Low	Medium	High
I don't move as much as I'd like to. I lead a pretty sedentary life.	I'm moderately active. I have a relatively active life.	I'm always on the go. I'm always on my feet. I never stop. I'm pretty active.

To talk about your eating habits you can say:

I eat everything.
I'm not a fussy eater; I eat most foods.

I don't eat meat.
I'm gluten-**intolerant**.
I follow a low-carb **diet**.
I try to avoid sugar.

I'm on a diet; if I follow this plan I should lose a kilo a week.
I'm a pretty fussy eater; there are many things I don't eat.
I'm intolerant to dairy produce; I'll feel ill if I eat/drink it.
I'm allergic to peanuts; I could have a bad reaction and may die if I eat them.

KEY TIP To sound more polite, you could use any of the above expressions after 'I'm sorry, but…' or 'I'm afraid…'.

Improve your vocabulary: *check new words using your dictionary app*

Some common types of diet	Useful words/phrases
standard diet	processed foods
pescatarian	junk food/fast food
vegetarian	whole foods
vegan	chemicals/additives
raw food	GMO *[Genetically Modified Organism]*
Paleo	preservatives
gluten-free	fad diet
balanced diet	organic food
clean eating	put on weight/lose weight

Leisure activities

To talk about your free time activities you can say:

I'm on a health kick at the moment; I'm eating well and exercising every day!
I'm addicted to exercise.
I do a lot of boxing.
I try to do exercise classes **as often as I can.**
I'm into weight training.
I'm a total yoga fanatic; I just love it!
I go to the gym every day.
I guess you can say **I'm a health nut;** I never drink or smoke and I exercise regularly.

I try to swim once or twice **a week.**
I want to meditate more, **but I lack motivation.**
I'm a real foodie; I love buying, cooking, eating and learning about good food.
I'm not really into exercise.
I hate getting sweaty.
I like hanging out with my friends, playing Xbox or **watching** football.
I suppose **I'm a couch potato;** I do spend most of my free time watching TV.
My weekly exercise is on Saturday nights, dancing with my friends.

I'm a social drinker/smoker; I only do it when I'm with friends.
I tend to binge drink at the weekends and drink nothing in the week.
I'm not an alcoholic, but I enjoy a nice glass of wine in the evening.
He's/She's a heavy drinker/smoker; he/she drinks/smokes a lot.
You could say I'm a party animal; I just love going out and dancing.
I'd say I'm a social butterfly; I like to spend time out and about with lots of different people.
I think **he's/she's got a problem with** drink.

Podcast conversation part 3

Tris:	So Reiss, how're you feeling?
Reiss:	A lot better than Saturday I can tell you!
Amanda:	So what did the doctors say?
Reiss:	Well, fortunately I haven't got cancer, which is great, but I have developed a big ulcer in my stomach, which has been causing me all the pain.
Tris:	That sounds awful mate. What caused it?
Reiss:	Well, the doctors can't be sure but they think it's probably lifestyle factors. They're going to try and cure it with diet changes first. They said I have to stop drinking coffee and alcohol, and I should try to include more fresh fruit and vegetables in my diet.
Amanda:	If I were you, I'd listen to them Reiss. You know how much changing my diet helped with my rheumatoid arthritis. Otherwise you might end up having an operation.
Reiss:	Yeah, but it's easier said than done! I was drinking eight cups of coffee a day before I came in here and I have to admit I'm a bit of a binge drinker. Then there's the junk food. They say I shouldn't have any take-aways, which is crazy as I can't cook! But if I don't do it, I might have to have an operation. What would you do if you were me Tris?
Tris:	If you want my opinion mate, I think you ought to do what the doctors say. I know I don't eat very well, so maybe I could support you and we can do it together.
Amanda:	That's a great idea! And we should start going for a walk at lunch times.
Reiss:	Yeah, thanks guys, I really appreciate your support.

Pronunciation

Listen to the conversation between Reiss, Amanda and Tris, then read each part out loud as you listen to the podcast. Try to copy their pronunciation. Listen again to podcast conversation 3 and how Amanda says 'If I were you…'. Focus on the stress: 'If **I** were **you**'.

Giving advice

When you want somebody to help you decide what to do you can ask:

What would you do in my position?
Can you give me some advice?
Do you have any words of wisdom for me?
What do you recommend?
What do you think I should do?
What do you reckon?

To give somebody advice you can say:

If I were you, I'd avoid sugar./**I'd** avoid sugar, **if I were you.**
If you ask me, you should try to be more active, maybe join a gym.
If you want my opinion, I think you should eat more vegetables.
You'd be better off if you stopped drinking so much wine!

! KEY TIP In English it is not correct to say 'if I was you'. Instead you should say 'if I were you' which is an irregular form from old English used for the second conditional form. For more on the conditional tense see Chapter 9.

Improve your vocabulary: *we use different phrases depending on how strong our opinion is*

Phrase	Meaning or strength of phrase
You have to…	*It's very important that you do this.*
You need to…	*It's important that you do this.*
You really ought to…	*It's a very good idea for you to do this.*
I think you should…	*It's a good idea for you to do this.*
You could always…	*It might be a good idea to do this.*
I don't think you should…	*It isn't a good idea to do this.*
You really shouldn't…	*It's a bad idea to do this.*
Whatever you do, don't…	*It's a very bad idea and you must not do this.*
You can't/mustn't…	*It's very important that you don't do this.*

Podcast conversation part 4

One year later.

Tris: So Reiss, are you ready for the marathon this weekend?

Reiss: Yeah, just need to pack my overnight bag. What about you?

Tris: Yep. Me too. You know, I can't believe how much our lives have changed over the last year!

Reiss: Tell me about it! I didn't think I'd still be alive, let alone living such a healthy lifestyle. We're so lucky Amanda knew so much about healthy living!

Tris: Too right! You know we should start a blog. I mean, if two middle-aged men can do this, anyone can! We could give advice on eating well, working out and being happy.

Reiss: One goal at a time mate. I'd focus on completing the marathon first if I were you!

Tris: Good point.

Time to Talk

1. Listen to all four parts of the podcast conversation between Amanda, Tris and Reiss at www.learnenglish2.eduaction. Notice their pronunciation then practise reading the dialogues. Record yourself on your phone then listen back. Do you sound like the speakers?
2. Use Siri/Cortana/voice recognition software to check your pronunciation of the vocabulary. If the voice recognition software can understand you, you're doing well!

Remember, the more you practise, the better you will be.

Grammar

G6 The past tenses

Look at the first two podcast conversations in this chapter and see how Amanda and Tris discuss the past.

- '**He went to hospital** yesterday and he was admitted'
  The past simple is used to describe a finished action in the past
- '**They were doing tests** when I spoke to him'
  The past continuous is used to describe an action in progress at that time
- '**Reiss hasn't been at work** this week'
  The present perfect simple is used to describe an action that started in past and is still true
- '**He's been acting a bit strangely** for a little while now'
  The present perfect continuous to describe an action that has been in progress for a period of time and is still happening now

Here's how the different past tenses are used

Past simple	**Present perfect simple**	**Past continuous**	**Present perfect continuous**
Focus on finished action. Used for state verbs. Used to describe a shorter or main action.	Focus on the result of action. Used for state verbs. Answers the question 'How many times....?'	Focus on the progress of an action. Not used for state verbs. Used to describe background actions	Focus on the action itself. Not used for state verbs. Answers the question 'How long...?'

To revise the form of the tenses, see the **Grammar guide** on pages 119–128.

5 Out and about

Speaking to strangers

To get somebody's attention in a polite way you can say:

Excuse me, could I just stop you for a second...
Excuse me, **I was wondering if you could help me?**
Excuse me, **do you have a minute?**
Sorry, could I just ask...
Sorry to bother you, but...
Sorry, I hope I'm not interrupting, but...

Then you can ask:

Would you mind telling me where the library is?
Do you happen to know when the museum opens?
Could you please tell me where the toilet is?
Do you know if there are any tickets left for this show?
Could I just ask what time the train leaves?
I don't suppose you know how long the bus takes?
I was just wondering what the time was?
Would you be able to tell me where I can find the eggs?
Do you think you could possibly move your car back a little bit?

Grammar
See G7 on indirect questions on page 49.

If somebody asks you a question you can answer:

I'm sorry, **I'm not from around here.**
I'm sorry, **I have no idea.**
I'm really sorry, **I'm in a hurry.**
I'm afraid I don't.
I'm not sure, but I think it's platform 3.
Ooh, good question, I think you go down the road and it's on the left.
I don't actually know, but if you ask at the Ticket Office they can help you.

Of course, it's almost half past three.
Absolutely, it's £14 for adults, £10 for children.
No problem, you just go downstairs and it's straight ahead.
Sure, you take bus 24 for six stops.

Podcast conversation part 1

Emily: Excuse me, I'm so sorry to bother you but I was wondering if you could help me; I'm looking for the Science Museum?

Fahed: I'm afraid I'm not from around here, but I think it's in that direction?

Emily: OK, thank you.

Emily: Sorry, could I just ask, do you happen to know where the Science Museum is?

Jo: Absolutely, you just go along here to the end then turn right. It's about 200 yards down there on the right.

Emily: Thank you so much, London is so confusing!

Jo: Do you mind me asking where you're from?

Emily: Not at all, I'm visiting from Devon.

Jo: Oh, wonderful. I used to go there on holiday when I was young, it's the best part of England if you ask me!

Emily: I agree, it's certainly less hectic than London, but London is lovely too.

Jo: I suppose so. Well, have a great day.

Emily: Thanks, you too.

Pronunciation

Listen to the conversation above, then practise reading it aloud and record yourself on your phone. Compare to the original, then repeat if necessary. Focus on the stress of the words and sentences.

Shopping

When a shop assistant asks if you need help you can say:

I'm actually looking for a birthday present for my son.
I'm trying to find the men's department.
I was wondering if you had any coffee machines?
I'm after some trainers.
I'm just browsing, thanks.
No, I'm fine thanks.

When you want to pay you can ask:

Do you take credit cards?
Is it OK to pay by debit card?
I assume you take cash?
I don't suppose you take American Express?
Can I pay by Apple Pay?
Do you accept PayPal?
Do you have contactless?
What's your **returns policy?**

You can also ask these questions using question tags (see Chapter 3):

You take credit cards, **don't you?**
You accept debit cards, **don't you?**
I can pay by PayPal here, **can't I?**
You've got contactless, **haven't you?**

KEY TIP

People often confuse 'pay' and 'buy'. Both verbs are used to talk about shopping, but 'pay' describes the action of giving your money to the shop and 'buy' describes the whole process of choosing the thing, paying for it and taking it home, e.g.

To a friend: *I need to buy some new shoes.*

In a shop: *Excuse me, where do I pay for these shoes?*

Podcast conversation part 2

In the Science Museum

Elaine: Are you alright there?

Emily: Yes, I'm fine, thanks.

2 minutes later

Emily: Excuse me, could you please tell me where I can find the gift shop?

Elaine: Of course, it's on the ground floor, next to the restaurant.

Emily: Thank you.

In the gift shop

Steve: Can I help you madam?

Emily: I hope so! I'm looking for a souvenir for my nephew. I don't suppose you could show me what you have?

Steve:	Of course, how old is he?
Emily:	He's seven, and he loves trains.
Steve:	Well, I think we have the perfect thing right over here. It's a 'build your own' steam locomotive, just like the one we have in the main hall.
Emily:	That sounds great, thank you. Where do I pay?
Steve:	I can do that for you just here.
Emily:	Excellent, thank you. How much is it?
Steve:	That'll be £24.99, please.
Emily:	I don't quite have the cash on me, I assume you take credit cards?
Steve:	Yes.
Emily:	OK, and have you got contactless?
Steve:	We have, we got it installed last year.
Emily:	Excellent... all done.
Steve:	And here's your receipt, just hold on to it in case you change your mind.
Emily:	Will do, thanks.
Steve:	Have a great afternoon.
Emily:	You too, bye.

Pronunciation

Listen to the conversation and read the script. Then read it aloud and record yourself on your smartphone. Listen to your recording and compare with the podcast. Repeat this until you are happy with your pronunciation.

If you have a problem and want to return something to the shop you can say:

I was wondering if I could return this, please.
I'd like a refund for this jacket please.
I'd like to get my money back, please.
Would it be possible to bring this book **back?**
I'd like to exchange this T-shirt, **please**, it's too small.

If they ask for your receipt or proof of purchase you can say:

Yes, here you go.

Actually it was a gift, but it's not quite what I wanted.
I'm afraid I've lost it.
Unfortunately not.

Pronunciation

Remember that receipt has a silent 'p'.

Improve your vocabulary: *check the meaning of any new words using your dictionary app*

Types of shops	Ways to pay	Types of transaction
department store internet shop/website/online shop independent shop chain store specialist shop antique shop charity shop[UK]/thrift store[US]	cash credit card Visa/American Express debit card PayPal/Apple Pay contactless gift voucher	purchase refund buy on credit/buy now, pay later put down a deposit pay the balance exchange sale

To talk about special prices you can say:

Is this chocolate **buy-one-get-one-free?**
Pay for one, get two.

Is this soup **on offer?**
Selling at a special price for a short period of time, e.g. 30% discount.

Are these earphones also **in the sale? [UK]**
Part of a seasonal promotional discount.

Is this necklace **on sale? [US]**
Part of a seasonal promotional discount.

Do you have any books **that are reduced?**
Selling for a lower price.

Is there any way you could do me a deal on that car?
Can you give me a special price?

This box **is damaged; do you think you could give me a discount?**
Asking for money off.

What's your best price for this?

Podcast conversation part 3

[In the Science Museum gift shop]

Emily: Excuse me, I bought this train for my nephew about 10 minutes ago, but I've changed my mind, I was wondering if I could exchange it for this T-shirt?

India: That shouldn't be a problem madam. Do you have your receipt?

Emily: Yes, here you go.

India: And you'd like to take the T-shirt instead, yes?

Emily: Yes, but I was wondering if you have another one as this one has a mark on the sleeve?

India: Oh, I see it. I assume there are no more on the shelf?

Emily: No, this was the last one in his size.

India: Unfortunately, we have no more in stock until Wednesday.

Emily: Oh, that's a shame. I mean it will probably come out in the wash I suppose.

India: Yes, I think it's just some dirt.

Emily: I don't suppose you'd be able to do me a small discount, would you?

India: Certainly, I can take 10% off for you. Would that be OK?

Emily: Yes, that's great, thank you.

India: OK, well if you can pass me your card, I'll process the refund and sale.

Emily: Thank you.

Pronunciation

Listen to the conversation and read the script. Practise Emily's part; read it aloud and record yourself on your smartphone. Listen to your recording and compare with the podcast. Repeat this until you are happy with your pronunciation.

Travelling around

To talk about your travel habits, you can say:

Personally, I prefer using public transport as it gives me time to read.
I believe that public transport's much greener than driving.
I used to drive **to work,** but I spent all my time in traffic jams!
The roads are so congested that the train is definitely the best option.
I love cycling to work, especially since the council put in all the cycle lanes.
I usually go to work on foot; walking is the best exercise!

I commute to work by bus.
Commute = travel to work in another place

You get a better price if you **buy train tickets in advance.**
In advance = before you travel

I have a season ticket for my journey to work.
Season ticket = a ticket for 1 month or 1 year

The trouble with public transport is that it's so unreliable.
I find public transport is too inconvenient and expensive.
I prefer the luxury of travelling by car; I don't need to worry about timetables.
I hate using public transport; it's too crowded and dirty.
I'm not a big fan of buses, but **I don't mind** taking the train.
I love being able to commute by plane **to work** in London and live in Barcelona.
While I agree that public transport **is** a more environmentally friendly option, **it's too** slow.
What I hate about train **travel is** standing on the platform in the cold when it's delayed.

See Chapter 9 for more phrases to express your opinion.

Improve your vocabulary: *check any new words using your dictionary app*

Train	General (bus/tram)	Air	Car
platform ticket inspector season ticket railcard coach buffet car sleeper train delay	ticket driver seat passengers stop terminal route request stop	customs hand luggage baggage allowance checked bags passport control cabin crew boarding pass short haul/long haul	petrol station [UK] gas station [US] brake *(stop)* clutch *(to change gear)* manual [UK], shift [US] accelerator *(to go faster)* flat tyre flat battery

Grammar
See G8 on prepositions *by*, *in* and *on* with forms of transport on page 50.

Podcast conversation part 4

Emily: Excuse me, sorry to bother you, but does this train go to Paddington?

Angel: No, you want the next one.

Emily: OK thanks.

At Paddington Station

Emily: Hi, I was wondering if you could help me. Which platform does the next train to Exeter depart from?

Ben: You want platform 10 in 25 minutes my love. Do you have a ticket?

Emily: Yes, I bought a return ticket, but I forgot my glasses so I can't read the information board!

Ben: That's not a problem. First class will be at the front of the train.

Emily: First class? I wish! Thank you for your help.

Ben: No trouble at all. There's a buffet car on the train if you need it.

Emily: Thank you.

25 minutes later

Emily: Sorry, but do you know when the train to Exeter will be arriving?

Ben:	I'm sorry, it's been delayed at Reading but it should be here in about 45 minutes.
Emily:	Should be?
Ben:	That's all the information I have at the moment.
Emily:	OK well, thanks anyway. I really must learn to drive; public transport can be so unreliable!

Time to Talk

1. Listen to all four of Emily's podcast conversations at www.learnenglish2.education. Notice the pronunciation and practise reading the dialogues. Record yourself on your phone then listen back. Do you sound like the speakers?
2. Use Siri/Cortana/voice recognition software to check your pronunciation of the vocabulary. If the voice recognition software can understand you, you're doing well!

Remember, the more you practise, the better you will be.

Grammar

G7 Indirect questions

Indirect questions are used when we want to be more polite, e.g. in a business meeting, with a stranger, or asking a friend for a favour.

Question phrase	**if/whether/question word/adverb***	**Affirmative phrase**
Would you mind telling me	if/whether	this is the way to the bus station?
Do you happen to know	if/whether	they take cards in here?
Could you please tell me	who	I need to speak to about studying here?
Do you know	what time	the train leaves?
Could I just ask	where	the nearest cash machine is?
I don't suppose you know	how much	a ticket costs?
I was just wondering	when	the cinema opens?
Would you be able to tell me	how long	the wait is?
Do you think you could	possibly	lend me your phone?

*We use if/whether for closed questions, question word for open questions, adverbs for polite requests.

G8 Prepositions by, in and on with forms of transport

It is easy to use the wrong prepositions when talking about forms of transport. The table below shows the correct ones to use.

by + all forms of transport	**in + most private transport**	**on + public transport**
car	a car	a train
train	a taxi	a bus/coach
bus	a helicopter	a tram
plane	a van	a plane
tram	a lorry [UK], truck [US]	the underground/metro/ subway
helicopter	a tuk tuk	
ferry		a ferry/boat
bike		
underground		
boat		**on** + transport that you sit on top of
tuk tuk		
		a motorbike
		a bike
		a horse
		on foot (singular) *(walking)*

6 In a restaurant

Booking a table

To reserve a table over the phone you can say:

I'd like to reserve a table for Saturday night, please.
I was wondering if I could book a table for tomorrow lunch time?
Do you have any tables available for Monday evening?
I'd like a table for Friday night, please.
Is it possible to book a table for Sunday, please.
I'd like to make a reservation for 13th June, please?
Would it be possible to book a table for Thursday evening?

What times do you have available?
What's the earliest/latest you can do?
Do you have anything a bit earlier/later?
Is 7 o'clock **OK?**
8.30**'s fine thanks.**
1 p.m. **is perfect, thank you.**
12.30 **it is, thank you.**

There'll be five **of us.**
For two, please.
At the moment it's for six, **but that might change.**
It's for eight.
There are seven **adults and a baby so we'll need a highchair, please.**

To make special requests you can ask:

Would it be possible to have a table by the window?
I don't suppose we could sit upstairs?
It's for a birthday party, so **I'd like to** arrange some decorations and a cake **if possible.**
One of our party is a wheelchair user, **so we'd like to have** a table with good access, **please.**
Do you think we could order a bottle of champagne for when we arrive?

Podcast conversation part 1

Asako: Good afternoon, Asako's kitchen. How can I help?

Julie: Hello, I was wondering if I could book a table for Saturday night?

Asako: This Saturday?

Julie: Yes, please.

Asako: OK. For how many people?

Julie: Well, at the moment there are eight of us, but that might change.

Asako: OK, we can add places if you let us know.

Julie: Of course.

Asako: What time would you like the table for?

Julie: Is 7.30 OK?

Asako: For eight people, I have a table available at 9?

Julie: Do you have anything a bit earlier?

Asako: I suppose I could move some tables and fit you in at 8?

Julie: 8's great, thank you.

Asako: OK. Is that everything?

Julie: Actually, it's for an engagement party, so if possible I'd like to arrange for a couple of bottles of champagne when we arrive?

Asako: That's no problem. And can I take a name?

Julie: Yes, it's Julie Smith.

Asako: Right, so that's a table for eight, at 8 o'clock, Saturday night with champagne. Anything else?

Julie: No, that's perfect, thank you.

Asako: You're welcome. See you on Saturday.

Julie: See you then; goodbye.

Asako: Goodbye.

Pronunciation

Listen to the conversation above, then practise reading Julie's part aloud and record yourself on your phone. Compare to the original, then repeat if necessary. Focus on the stress of the words and sentences.

Ordering your food

If you have questions about the ingredients you can ask:

Could you tell me if there's garlic **in the** soup?
Is the cannelloni **suitable for vegetarians**?
What do you have that's gluten free?
Do you know if the pie **contains** onion?
Could I just ask if the chicken is free range?
I'm allergic to milk. **Would you mind asking the chef if it's in** the steak sauce?

If you want to make changes to the menu you can say:

I'll have the sea bass **please, but could I swap the** chips [UK]/fries [US] for salad?
I'd like the steak **please, but can you make sure it's** extra rare?
Can I have the chicken, **but without** cheese, **please?**
Would it be possible to have the risotto with mushroom **instead of** asparagus?
I don't suppose I could order the soup, **but change the** bread for chips [UK]/fries[US]?
I'll take the quinoa salad, **but could I have the** dressing **on the side, please?**
Sorry to be a pain, but could I order a smaller portion?
I don't mean to be difficult, but do you have sweet potato fries?
Is there any way I could have the mushrooms **cooked in** olive oil, **rather than** butter?

Grammar

See G9 on how to use 'but' on page 58.

Podcast conversation part 2

In the restaurant

Ikumi:	Are you ready to order?
Julie:	I think so, yes, but I have a couple of questions.
Ikumi:	Yes?
Julie:	Is the tempura suitable for vegans?
Ikumi:	No, I'm afraid not; we use egg in the batter.
Julie:	OK, do you know if the spring rolls contain meat?
Ikumi:	No, they're suitable for vegetarians and vegans.
Julie:	Excellent, then I'll have the spring rolls to start, but could I swap the sweet chilli sauce for soy sauce?
Ikumi:	Of course. And what would you like for your main course?
Julie:	I really don't mean to be difficult, but could you ask the chef if there are peanuts in this dish?
Ikumi:	Certainly, I'll be right back.
2 minutes	
Ikumi:	Hi, I'm afraid there are peanuts in that dish, but this one is OK for vegans and has no peanuts.
Julie:	Thank you so much. Is there any way I could have it with noodles instead of rice?
Ikumi:	Yes, of course.
Julie:	Great. Then I'll have that. And could I have another glass of wine, please?
Ikumi:	Yes, I'll get that for you right away.
Julie:	Thank you so much.

Pronunciation

Listen to the conversation and read the script. Notice how the tone of Julie's voice becomes softer when she is being 'difficult' and asking to change the menu. This shows that the other person has the power but you want them to be nice to you. Repeat Julie's part and record yourself. Listen back. Do you sound like you are giving an order or asking for a favour?

Talking about your meal

To make comments on your food you can say:

This steak **is** excellent.
I'm really enjoying this.
You should have ordered this pie, **it's** incredible.
I'm not keen on curry **in general, but this is** delicious.
The fish **is a little** spicy **for me.**
I'm not very impressed by the chicken.
I think there's too much cheese on this pasta.
I can't say this is the best burger **in town, but it's** quite nice.

Improve your vocabulary: *check the meaning of new words using your dictionary app*

Taste		
Positive	**Neutral**	**Negative**
delicious [NG, extreme] refreshing tasty flavourful scrumptious [NG, extreme]	mild strong spicy fruity tangy sweet savoury	tasteless [NG, absolute] bland overpowering acidic bitter sour salty

Texture		
Positive	**Neutral**	**Negative**
cooked to perfection [NG, absolute] tender light juicy creamy succulent rich	moist gooey crispy crumbly crunchy chewy smooth	overdone/undercooked dry tough stodgy raw [NG, absolute] stringy greasy

Grammar
Remember in Chapter 1 we looked at gradable and non-gradable adjectives (see page 9). The table above shows which adejctives are non-gradable (NG) and notes whether these adjectives are absolute or extreme.

Making a complaint

KEY TIP When you are complaining, wherever you are, try to **be polite**! You want the other person to help you, so being angry with them isn't a good idea.

To make a complaint you can say:

Excuse me, there seems to have been a mistake; I ordered fish **and you've given me** beef.
Sorry, but I think there's been a mix up; I asked for soup, **not** salad.
I'm sorry but I think there's some confusion; I wanted my steak rare **and this is** well done.
Sorry to be a pain, but my chicken's cold.
Excuse me, I don't like to complain, but this brownie **is** burnt.

If the problem isn't solved you can say:

I'm sorry but **I can't eat that.**

I'd like a refund, please.
If you've already paid.
I'm afraid I won't be paying for that.
If you haven't paid yet.

Would it be possible to speak to the manager, please?
I'd like to speak to whoever's in charge, please.

I'm afraid **that's unacceptable.**
I can't believe that you're serving raw fish in this restaurant.
I'm sorry, but **it's just not good enough.**
I have to say, **I'm incredibly disappointed.**

Podcast conversation part 3

Julie: Excuse me?

Ikumi: Yes?

Julie: There seems to have been a mistake. I ordered vegetarian spring rolls and these have greasy meat in them.

Ikumi: I'm very sorry; I'll get that changed for you.

Julie: Thank you.

2 minutes later

Ikumi: Here you go madam.

Julie: Thank you. Let me just see... No, look, this has meat in as well. I'm sorry but I can't eat that.

Ikumi: I'm so sorry. I'll take it back to the kitchen.

Julie: Could I speak to the manager, please?

Ikumi: Of course, I'll get her for you.

2 minutes later

Asako: Hello madam, how can I help you?

Julie: Well, there seems to have been some confusion over the spring rolls. I ordered vegetarian and twice you've given me meat ones! I'm afraid that's unacceptable.

Asako: No, madam, I assure you it's not meat, it's soy protein.

Julie: I've never seen soy protein that is fatty and greasy like that! I'm sorry but I won't be paying for it, and I'd like to cancel my order, please.

Asako: Of course, madam. Will you still be having your main course?

Julie: Yes, please.

Pronunciation

Listen to the conversation and read the script. Listen to when she's complaining, Julie is polite, but firm. Practise saying the phrases above in this voice – somewhere between asking a favour and being angry.

Paying the bill

When you want to pay the bill you can say:

Could I have the bill, please? **[UK]**
Could I get the check, please? **[US]**
I'd like to settle up, please.
Is it OK to get the bill, please?
Just the check, thanks.

Podcast conversation part 4

Ikumi: Will there be anything else, madam?

Julie: No, just the bill, thanks.

Ikumi: Of course, madam.

2 minutes later

Ikumi: Here you are madam.

Julie: Thank you. Do you take American Express?

Ikumi: I'm afraid not, but we take all other credit cards.

Julie: OK, well here you go.

Ikumi: Thank you, and once again I'm so sorry for earlier. Please accept a cup of coffee, on the house.

Julie: Well, thank you very much.

Time to Talk

1. Listen to all four parts of the podcast conversation between Julie, Asako and Ikumi at www.learnenglish2.education. Notice their pronunciation then practise reading the dialogues. Record yourself on your phone then listen back. Do you sound like the speakers?
2. Use Siri/Cortana/voice recognition software to check your pronunciation of the vocabulary. If the voice recognition software can understand you, you are doing well!

Remember, the more you practise, the better you will be.

Grammar

G9 The '+ but structure'

When we want to be 'difficult', we use the **'+ but'** structure where the first part of the sentence is positive, and we use **but** to introduce the second negative part – the part the other person doesn't want to hear, e.g. *I'll take the quinoa salad, but could I have the dressing on the side, please?*

7 At work

Talking about work

To talk about your job you can say:

I've applied for several jobs; I hope I get one of them.
I've got a job interview tomorrow.

I've got a new job.
I've been offered a job working for UNICEF.
I've just started a new job.
I've just been promoted to manager of my department.

I work full/part-time.
I run my own business.
I'm self-employed.
I work from home.

I work for a big company.
I work in a hospital
I work in the fashion industry.
At the moment I'm working on a big project.
I mostly do office work and administration, **but there's an element of** customer service.
I spend a lot of time in meetings.
My job's difficult to explain.
I'm responsible for the logistics of our company.
I mainly organise the staff rotas and pay invoices.
I love my job. **I work with a great team** and every day is different.

I'm currently unemployed so I'm looking for work.
I recently lost my job.
My company was downsizing and **they let me go.**
I was made redundant; my job doesn't exist anymore.
I was fired because my boss said I was lazy.

Improve your vocabulary: *check any new words using your dictionary app*

Companies	Career	Benefits	Business
CEO (Chief Executive Officer) department HR (Human Resources) line manager team leader board of directors	promotion pay increase career ladder redundancy made redundant get fired retire	paid holiday company car health insurance expense account sick pay bonus	presentation meeting deal conference consultant contractor

For more work related vocabulary see http://learnenglish.britishcouncil.org/en/business-and-work

Podcast conversation part 1

Mohammed: Hi, Geva. Did you have that meeting with your department manager yesterday?

Geva: Hey, Mohammed, yes I did. He told me about the restructuring.

Mohammed: Oh? How did it go?

Geva: Well, technically he fired me!

Mohammed: Really? Oh dear!

Geva: Yeah, I kind of thought the same, but then he offered me another job, so it's fine. My department is disappearing, so they want me to be the head of a new department.

Mohammed: And what do you think about that?

Geva: Well, at first I was a bit annoyed, but actually this is kind of a promotion, and I have good benefits, so I can't complain.

Mohammed: Oh yeah?

Geva: Yeah, no more working with my old line manager!

Mohammed: Haha, well that's good.

Geva:	Exactly, and on top of that I get a company car, a bit of a pay rise, I can work from home 4 days a week, and I have to travel 1 week a month for meetings with our international clients, so I'm pretty excited, actually.
Mohammed:	That sounds great! Congratulations!
Geva:	Thanks.

Pronunciation

Listen to the conversation above, then practise reading Geva's part aloud and record yourself on your phone. Compare to the original, then repeat if necessary. Focus on the stress of the words and sentences.

Giving instructions

Whether you are the boss or not, sometimes you need to give instructions, but if we want people to do things in a work setting, it's important to be polite.

You can say:

Would you be able to take this to the post room [UK]/mail room [US]?
I'd like you to make ten copies, please.
Could you please turn the photocopier on?
If you could give that to John, **that'd be great.**
If you wouldn't mind working with Heidi?
Can I leave it with you?
Do you think you could e-mail me with the numbers by the end of today?
Would you mind finishing the report alone?

Grammar
See G10 on modal verbs on page 68.

Pronunciation

Even if instructions are in question form, you need to use a tone of voice to show that what you are saying is an instruction and not a question, so your voice should go down at the end.

Compare on the podcast below; the sentence is the same but the first is a question; the second, an instruction. Repeat the questions using your voice to show meaning.

Podcast for pronunciation

1 Can I leave it with you?

2 Can I leave it with you?

3 Would you be able to take this to the mail room?

4 Would you be able to take this to the mail room?

5 If you wouldn't mind working with Heidi?

6 If you wouldn't mind working with Heidi?

In some situations it is necessary to give more direct/stronger instructions, e.g. to a large number of people, or if you are in a position of high power. **In this case, you use the imperative:**

Be there at 8 a.m!
Leave your bag at the door!
Don't talk during the performance!

Grammar
See G11 on the imperative on page 68.

Pronunciation

The difference between the order and the advice is heard in your voice as well as the language used. You can make a direct instruction into an order by changing your voice. Try saying each sentence in a strong then a soft voice. Record yourself. Can you hear the difference between the instruction and the advice?

To make the imperative a little more polite, you can say:

Lock the doors when you leave, **please.**
Put the files in alphabetical order, **please.**
Do clean the kitchen thoroughly.
Do tell me when it's finished.

Podcast conversation part 2

Geva:	And what about you, Mohammed? How did your meeting go?
Mohammed:	Not as well as yours! I've been moved to another department and my new boss is from Russia. She's nice but there's a big cultural difference.
Geva:	What do you mean?
Mohammed:	Well, her English isn't brilliant, so she's much more direct than I'm used to, even than Todd, the Australian guy we worked for 8 years ago.
Geva:	Wow, I remember Todd!
Mohammed:	Yeah, well, Natalia always sounds like a sergeant in the army giving orders!
Geva:	Oh dear.
Mohammed:	Yesterday for example, she wanted me to help her understand the sales for last month, which isn't part of my job, and she said 'Mohammed, explain this to me!' no 'please' or 'would you mind' just 'explain this'.
Geva:	That sounds horrible.
Mohammed:	It is, I was really angry, but I have to remind myself that she doesn't mean to be rude.
Geva:	Try not to take it personally, and I'm sure she will get more polite as her English improves!
Mohammed:	I really hope so!

Pronunciation

Listen to the conversation and read the script. Read both Geva and Mohammed's parts and record yourself on your phone. Listen back.

Making it clear

Sometimes we say something but people may misunderstand.

If you are not sure you understand what somebody is saying you can say 'I'm sorry' followed by:

I'm not sure I follow; are you suggesting that we go ahead?
Do you mean you don't want to take on that project?
What exactly are you saying?
What do you mean by 'creative'?
Can I just check that I understand what you're saying?
I'm hearing that you think it's a good idea?
Could you just explain what you mean when you say it's an interesting idea?
So are you saying that we should go ahead?
Do you want me to send the e-mail or not?
Can I just check that we're on the same page; what you mean is we need to close?
So, to clarify, you're saying that we have to fire 100 people?

To make sure somebody understands you, you can say:

What I mean is, I think we should cancel the deal.
To put it another way, I think we should try something different.
To clarify, I don't recommend doing that.
Actually, I was saying the opposite.
In other words, we should consider other options.
To put it simply, I'm saying that we have to make a decision today.
What I was trying to say was that I believe it's a dangerous move.
I said I wasn't sure if it's a good idea, **which means** I think it's a bad idea!
When I said to hold off on that, **I was asking you** not to reply to the e-mail.

! KEY TIP

These phrases can be used in any conversation when you want to make sure the conversation is understood clearly. Don't be afraid to ask someone what they really mean if you are not quite sure. English speakers often use idioms when they speak and these can be confusing, so when you don't know, use this language to ask what they mean.

Podcast conversation part 3

A few months later

Geva: So, moving on to the new deal. What do you have to report back to me?

Mohammed: Well, looking at the figures I'd say there's room for improvement, or, to put it another way, I think we need to renegotiate with them.

Geva: I'm sorry, are you saying that the past 3 months have been a waste of time?

Mohammed: Actually, I'm saying the opposite. The past 3 months have given me time to analyse the market while you were negotiating with them, and I'm glad, because if you look here…

Pause

Geva: OK, so could you explain what you mean by renegotiate?

Mohammed: Yes, what I mean is, I think we could easily ask for another 3%, maybe even 5.

Geva: So to clarify, do you mean 5% more than we've already agreed, or 5% on top of their original number?

Mohammed: 5% on top of what we've already agreed, and that's not the only thing; we can also get them to invest an extra 10% on this part of the agreement if you look at these projections here.

Geva: I'm not sure I follow.

Mohammed: To put it simply, if this goes the way I think it will, they'll be happy to invest the extra as the profits will be huge.

Geva: Right, well, thank you Mohammed. I'll get on the phone to Seoul and see what I can do.

Pronunciation

Listen to the conversation and read the script. First focus on Geva's part, then Mohammed's. Listen to their intonation when they use the clarification language. Pausing is very important to give the person listening, time to understand. Practise saying their lines using the pauses and intonation. Record yourself and compare to the podcast.

Giving feedback

Some phrases in English have a different meaning when used for feedback, and in a work environment it is useful to be able to 'read between the lines'.

Improve your vocabulary

What we say	What we mean
That's not bad.	That's good.
That's pretty good.	That's very good.
I'm not sure about that idea.	I don't like the idea at all.
I'll bear it in mind.	I won't remember it.
It's not quite what I was looking for.	It's rubbish. Start again.
I have a few other options to consider.	I won't be using your idea.
I've made a couple of comments.	I've made a lot of corrections.
It's not your best work.	It's not very good at all.
It's not brilliant.	It's quite bad.
It's an interesting idea.	It's a stupid idea.
The idea has some positives.	I hate it.
That's a brave plan.	You're crazy.

To tell somebody you are happy with their work be specific. You can say:

I really liked how you included everyone in the project.
I thought it was great when you showed us the short film in the presentation.
I was impressed by the way you dealt with that customer.
I particularly liked how you presented the new logo to music.
The visual aids in your presentation **were excellent.**

If you need to give negative feedback, try to avoid saying 'you'. You can say:

I noticed that there **were no suggestions for improvement in the proposal.**
It seemed to me that the report lacked a lot of information.
I got the impression that the project wasn't quite finished.

Then finish with a constructive solution (how can they improve). You can say:

Perhaps next time more attention should be paid to the finances.
You could try including more visual aids next time.
It might be an idea to speak more slowly.
In future I would suggest sending emails to everyone involved.
Maybe next time you could work with somebody else to bounce ideas off each other.

Podcast conversation part 4

Geva:	Hi Mohammed, do you have a minute?
Mohammed:	Of course, what can I do for you?
Geva:	I just wanted to give you some feedback about our meeting last week.
Mohammed:	Sure.
Geva:	Well, to start with, thank you so much for all your hard work. That report was a great tool for me in my renegotiations with the company.
Mohammed:	My pleasure.
Geva:	But I noticed that the report didn't focus on the African market and I was wondering why not?
Mohammed:	To be honest, I didn't have time to get the information together as we only had a small team.
Geva:	Aah. OK, well perhaps next time you could let us know that you need more people?
Mohammed:	Of course, and thank you for the feedback.

Time to Talk

1. Listen to all four parts of the podcast conversation between Geva and Mohammed at www.learnenglish2.com. Notice their pronunciation then practise reading the dialogues. Record yourself on your phone then listen back. Do you sound like the speakers?
2. Use Siri/Cortana/voice recognition software to check your pronunciation of the vocabulary. If the voice recognition software can understand you, you are doing well!

Remember, the more you practise, the better you will be.

Grammar

G10 Modal verbs in questions and instructions

Notice that when modal verbs are used for questions or instructions, less formal phrases use the present tense, more formal use the past:

Informal	Example	Formal	Example
can	I can do that for you.	could	I could do that for you.
will	Will you explain this please.	would	Would you explain this please.
may	May I use your desk?	might	Might I use your desk?

G11 The imperative

The imperative uses the bare infinitive of the verb to give instructions and orders. No subject is used.

It is used to give instructions and orders:

Give it to me!
Tidy your desk!
Send all e-mails before 4 p.m!
Park your cars carefully.

It is also used to give friendly advice:

Don't listen to him.
Try as hard as you can.
Ask for help if you need it.
Tell me if it's too much.

8 Using the phone

Making contact

Speaking to people face to face is one thing, but over the phone it can be more difficult. The phone has its own vocabulary which you need to know to communicate effectively.

To answer the phone at work you can say:

Good morning/afternoon Sarah **speaking. How can I help you?**
Jason's Company, Jason **speaking. How can I help?**
Hello, you're through to Big Bank. **What can I do for you today?**

> **! KEY TIP** If it's a personal call, you can answer simply 'Hello'.

To ask for the caller's name you can say:

Can I ask who's calling?
Could I take your name, please?
If I could just take your name?
Sorry, I didn't catch your name?

> **! KEY TIP** For friends you could say, 'Is that Eszter?', which is much less formal.

If you want to speak to someone in particular you can say:

Less formal	Formal - first time you speak
I was hoping to speak to Caroline **if she's about?** **I don't suppose** Valerie's **there is she?** **Can I speak to** Lorena **please?** **I'm calling for** Mr Pascoe.	**I was wondering if I could speak to** Jo, **please.** **I'd like to be connected to** Abdul's **office please.** **Would it be possible to speak to** Yejin **please?** **Could you put me through to** somebody in Marketing **please?**

To ask somebody to wait, you can say:

Could you **hold the line, please?**
Please hold the line while I try to connect you.
Bear with me and I'll put you through.
If you could just hold on one second I'll see if he's/she's in.
I'm just going to put you on hold for a second.
Please hold.

To say somebody isn't available you can say:

First	Followed by
I'm afraid he's/she's **just stepped out.** I'm sorry, he's/she's **in a meeting at the moment.** **I'm afraid he's/she's unavailable right now.** I'm sorry, he's/she's **on the other line.**	**Can I take a message?** **Would you like to leave a message?** **Can I help at all?** **Can I get** him/her **to call you back?**

To ask to leave a message (if the other person doesn't offer) you can say:

Would it be possible to leave a message?
Could I please leave a message?
Would you mind taking a message for me?
I don't suppose I could leave a message, could I?
Could you please ask him/her to call me back as soon as possible?

If you prefer not to leave a message you can say:

Do you happen to know when s/he'll be back?
Do you have any idea when s/he'll be free?
When would be a good time to call back?

It's OK, I'll call back this afternoon.
Not a problem, I'll try again later.
That's OK, I'll e-mail him/her.
Not to worry, I'll try his/her mobile [UK]/cell phone [US].
Thanks anyway, I'll just call back later.

Podcast conversation part 1

Phone rings

Jon:	Good Morning Oxford Composites, Jon speaking. How can I help?
Trish:	Good morning Jon. I was wondering if you could put me through to Alison in Accounts, please.
Jon:	Of course, could I just take your name please?
Trish:	Certainly. It's Trish Fisher.
Jon:	OK, could you just hold on for a second and I'll see if I can put you through.
Trish:	Thank you so much.

1 minute later

Jon:	Hello?
Trish:	Yes, I'm still here.
Jon:	Hi, I'm afraid there's nobody available in Accounts at the moment. Would you like to leave a message?
Trish:	Thanks, but it's quite complicated, I need to speak to them really. Do you know when would be a good time to call back?
Jon:	You could try again this afternoon, at about half past two GMT?
Trish:	OK, great, I'll do that and thank you for your time.
Jon:	Thank you, goodbye.

Pronunciation

Listen to the conversation above, then practise reading each part aloud and record yourself on your phone. Compare to the original, then repeat if necessary. Focus on the stress of the words and sentences.

Grammar
See G12 on phrasal verbs on page 76.

Phone problems

If you can't hear the other person very well you can say:

I'm sorry, **you're breaking up.**
Could you speak up? I can't quite hear you.
I'm afraid **this is a really bad line.** Can I call you back?
I've got really bad reception. Can I call you back in ten minutes?
Sorry, I didn't catch that, could you say it again?
This is a terrible connection, can I call you back?

If you think you may lose the connection you can say:

I'm afraid **I haven't got much signal.**
I'm on a train and **I'm about to go through a tunnel.**
My battery is really low so we might get cut off.
I'm just about to go into the subway **so I may lose you.**
I think my phone is about to die. Can I call you from the office?

Podcast conversation part 2

Phone rings.

Jon: Good afternoon Oxford Composites, Jon speaking. How can I help?

Trish: Good Afternoon Jon...

Jon: I'm sorry, I didn't catch that, you're breaking up. Could you say it again?

Trish: I said...

Jon: I'm really sorry, but this is a terrible line, I can't hear a thing. Would you mind calling back?

Trish: Sure.

Phone rings again

Jon: Good afternoon Oxford Composites, Jon speaking. How can I help?

Trish: Good afternoon Jon, Trish here again. Is that better?

Jon: Hello Trish, yes, it's still not great, but I can just about hear you now. What can I do for you?

Trish: I'd like to speak to Alison in Accounts please?

Jon: Of course, please hold the line and I'll try to put you through.

Trish: OK, but please don't be too long, my battery is low and we might get cut off.

Jon: OK I'll be as quick as I can.

Trish: Thank you.

A minute later

Jon: Trish, I'm so sorry, it's going straight to voicemail. Would you still like me to put you through?

Trish: I suppose I don't have a choice. Yes, please.

Pronunciation

Listen to the conversation and read the script. Read both Trish and Jon's parts and record yourself on your phone. Listen back.

Leaving a voicemail message

Most people dislike leaving voicemail messages, especially in another language, but to do it successfully follow the tips below.

First say who you are. You can say:

This is Brad Jones **calling for** Priti Patel.
Jin Hee Park **here, calling for** Jean-Claude.
It's Nick Pearman **calling for** Matthew Donovan.

Second say why you are calling. You can say:

I'm calling to discuss tomorrow's meeting.
I just wanted to let you know that I will be late for work tomorrow.
I'm just returning your call.
I'm just calling to tell you I'll be out of the office for the next 2 days.
Just to let you know, the delivery arrived this morning.
Just to say thank you for yesterday's presentation.

Third say what you want the other person to do. You can say:

Could you please call me back when you get this?
If you could send it by e-mail, **that'd be great.**
Can you call me back **as soon as possible?**
There's no need to call me back.
I'd like you to call me as soon as possible.

Finally leave your contact details. You can say:

You can reach me on 07977 733 765.

You have my number.

I think you have my details, but just in case, my number is 555 567 890.

My e-mail is TRISH@GMAIL.COM

Improve your vocabulary: *giving contact details over the phone*

@	at
-	hyphen
_	underscore
!	exclamation mark
.	dot
/	forward slash
0	zero or 'Oh'
33	'double 3'
555	'triple 5'

Use your pronunciation app to check the names of the letters as many people confuse the vowels and other letters like *g* and *j*; *u*, *v* and *w*; *y* etc.

Pronunciation

Speak slowly and clearly when you are leaving a message so that the other person does not have to listen to it several times to hear all of the information. Practise saying your phone number and e-mail address. Use your voice recognition app to see if you can say it correctly.

Podcast conversation part 3

Voicemail: You've reached the Accounts Department at Oxford Composites. I'm afraid there's nobody available to take your call right now, but if you leave your name, number and a short message after the beep we'll get back to you as soon as possible. Thank you.

Trish: Good afternoon, this is Trish Fisher calling for Alison Short. Just to let you know that I'll be flying into London tomorrow and I'll be in the UK for 5 days if you'd like to meet in person to discuss our account. If you could call me back after I land on Thursday, that'd be great. I think you already have my number but just in case, it's 01 234 5567. Thank you.

Pronunciation

Listen to Trish's message and how she speaks slowly and clearly. Practise leaving messages and record yourself on your phone.

Arranging a meeting

To arrange a meeting you can ask:

Would you be available to meet with me on Friday afternoon?
Would it be possible to get together on Monday to discuss it further?
Would you like to meet in person at my office to look at the plans?
Are you free on Tuesday morning?
Could we maybe do lunch on Wednesday, to talk it over?
Does Monday afternoon **work for you?**
Is Saturday morning any good for you?
I have a window on Tuesday lunchtime **if that's any good for you?**
How about dinner on Friday? We could finalise the deal then.

Podcast conversation part 4

Phone rings

Trish: Hello, Trish Fisher speaking.

Alison: Oh, hello Trish, it's Alison Short here calling from Oxford Composites.

Trish: Hello Alison, thank you for getting back to me.

Alison: Not a problem, I'm sorry I was tied up all day on Tuesday. How was the flight?

Trish: Yeah, not too bad, thank you. So Alison, would it be possible for us to get together sometime this week to discuss my account?

Alison: Absolutely. I've got a pretty free schedule, so when is good for you?

Trish: Well, I have a window tomorrow afternoon if that's any good for you?

Alison: Yep, I can do that. Would you like to come to the office at say 3?

Trish: Perfect, I look forward to it. See you then.

Time to Talk

1. Listen to all four parts of the podcast conversation between Trish, Jon and Alison at www.learnenglish2.education. Notice their pronunciation then practise reading the dialogues. Record yourself on your phone then listen back. Do you sound like the speakers?
2. Use Siri/Cortana/voice recognition software to check your pronunciation of the vocabulary. If the voice recognition software can understand you, you are doing well!

Remember, the more you practise, the better you will be.

Grammar

G12 Phrasal verbs

English has a lot of phrasal verbs. They can be difficult to learn, so try to remember just a few at a time.

Some phrasal verbs can be separated, e.g. ***put*** *somebody* ***through***, and some can't, e.g. ***hold on***.

You will notice on your dictionary app that separable phrasal verbs are usually written in the separated form to help you remember. When you learn the verb, if it can be separated, learn it that way.

Below are some phrasal verbs that are used for phone calls.

Phrasal verb		Meaning
pick up	=	answer the phone
put somebody through	=	connect somebody
hold on	=	wait
hang on	=	wait
get through to somebody	=	be connected to somebody
break up	=	losing signal so it is hard to hear the other person
speak up	=	speak more loudly
be cut off	=	lose connection on a call
hang up	=	end a phone call
put the phone down	=	end a phone call
ring/call somebody back	=	return a call to somebody who tried to call you
ring/call back later	=	try to call again later
get back to	=	call somebody back later on

Pronunciation

Type the phrasal verbs into your dictionary app and listen to where the stress is. Practise saying them in this way.

9 Having discussions

Speaking to people about topics you disagree on can be difficult. This chapter looks at ways to have difficult discussions without offending people.

Disagreeing politely

When you don't agree with what somebody is saying you can say:

I'm sorry, but that's not my experience.
I'm afraid I can't agree with that.

You can use the phrases below after **I'm sorry** but, or **I'm afraid** to soften them, or on their own.

Mild disagreement	Medium	Strong disagreement
I'm not sure about that. I wouldn't necessarily put it that way. I'm not convinced by that. I wouldn't say so. That's not my experience.	I have to disagree. I don't think that's right. I disagree. I can't agree with that.	I completely disagree! That's just not true! I don't see how you can say that! That's rubbish! That's nonsense!

Podcast conversation part 1

A couple is travelling in Thailand and trying to decide where to go next.

Juan: Well, I think that we should spend another few days in Bangkok. It's great here.

Laura: I'm not sure about that. I mean, Thailand is such a big country and we only have a month here. I think we should get going and head north to Chang Mai.

Juan: I'm afraid I disagree. A month is a long time and we still have a lot of things to see in Bangkok!

Laura: I'm sorry, but I have to disagree. We've been to all of the temples and palaces and museums that we had on our list. It's time to move on. There's nothing else I want to see here.

Juan: How can you say that? There is so much we haven't seen yet!

Laura: Juan, we aren't going to be able to see every single sight in every single place we visit.

Juan: I'm sorry, but I completely disagree; if we plan well we can see almost everything we want to see.

Laura: That's rubbish. We cannot see every sight in every city in Thailand in a single month!

Juan: Nonsense, we can if we plan!

Pronunciation

Listen to the conversation above. Focus on how Juan's and Laura's voices start gently, but then become stronger as the disagreement gets stronger. Practise reading each part aloud and record yourself on your phone. Compare to the original, and repeat if necessary.

Interrupting

To interrupt when somebody is speaking you can say:

I'm sorry, could I just cut in for a second? I'd just like to say I think that's a bad idea.
Sorry to interrupt, but could you speak up a bit please?
I don't mean to be rude, but could I talk to you for a second.
Please excuse the interruption, but I have to question that point.
Could I just interject? We have to remember the residents when we make this decision.
Do you mind if I just say, that those numbers are wildly inaccurate.
Could I just say something, please? I'm not sure this is necessarily true.
I'm sorry, but could I speak for a second? Despite what he's saying, I think we need to wait.

Preventing interruption

When somebody tries to interrupt you but you want to continue speaking you can say:

Do you mind if I just finish? As I was saying, this is the best plan.
Sorry, I haven't finished yet. Where was I? Oh, yes, the profit margin.
I've almost finished, I just wanted to add that Henry is in agreement with me.

Could you please wait until I have finished? Back to the action plan; we can start Tuesday.
If I could just finish what I was saying? And that's why we have to do this now.
I'm sorry, I'm still speaking. Anyway, that's what I'd suggest.

Notice the phrases we use to return to our conversation after an interruption, you can say:

Now where was I?
What was I saying?
Back to...
As I was saying, ...
Anyway, ...
Sorry about that, so...

Podcast conversation part 2

Juan:	Hey Laura, come and meet Taylor and Scott. They're from Scotland and are here for the same amount of time as we are.
Laura:	Hi, nice to meet you. Sorry to interrupt, but do you mind if I speak to Juan for a minute?
Juan:	Sorry Laura, I was just saying to these guys that...
Laura:	I don't mean to be rude, but I really need to talk to Juan.
Juan:	Do you mind if I just finish? So, as I was saying, I've been reading in the guide book about a temple where we can touch tigers. It's not too...
Laura:	Please excuse the interruption guys, but I have to talk to Juan now.
Juan:	Laura, I'm still speaking! Anyway, it's about 2 hours from here and we can get a bus there and back...
Laura:	Juan, this is really important.
Juan:	Just give me a minute, I'm in the middle of a conversation here!
Laura:	Juan, your brother has been in a car crash and he's in hospital!

Pronunciation

Listen to the conversation and read the script. Focus on how Juan and Laura use their voices when they interrupt (softer, more polite), or try to stop interruptions (stronger). Read both parts and record yourself on your phone. Listen back.

Persuading people

To persuade people to consider your idea you can say:

But don't you think we ought to consider the impact on the environment?
Wouldn't it be better to wait for the report first?
I really think we need to take this into account.
Have you thought about how this will look to the public?
I think it's important to use all of our resources.
If you ask me we ought to buy it.
It's obviously best to wait a little bit longer.
I think it's vital that we hire some more people.
Look, we need the money, they need the workers, **it makes sense to** sub-contract.

To disagree with and then persuade people you can say:

I can see your point, but don't you think it would be better if we have lunch first?
You may be right, but wouldn't you say it's a risky idea?
I can see why you'd say that, but if you think about it from his/her point of view, it's fine.
I understand where you're coming from, but I just think the other plan is better.
While what you're saying is partially true, do you honestly believe that they won't come?

Explaining why you are right.

When we want to persuade people that we are right, it is good to give an example of a possible result to show why we think that. This means we need to talk about **hypothetical situations** which are likely or not so likely to happen. Look at the examples below:

If we buy that house, we will have no money.
1st conditional; possible future situation

If we bought that house, we would have no money left.
2nd conditional; hypothetical or unlikely future situation

If we had bought that house, we would have had no money for our holiday.
3rd conditional; hypothetical past situation, can't be changed

Grammar
See G13 on conditional tenses on page 85.

To argue your point using this language you can say:

If we go to the cinema, **we'll** miss the last train home.
If Germany wins the game, the Greek fans **won't be** happy.
You'll lose your job **if you**'re late for work again.

If we took the later train, **we'd** save money and still arrive on time.
You could buy a new computer **if you** sold me your old one.
If we got a dog, **it would** protect the house from burglars.

You wouldn't have got that job **if I hadn't** helped you write your CV!
If we'd gone the way I suggested, **we would have** arrived by now.

If you'd booked a table like I asked you to, **we'd be** eating in the restaurant now.

When you are being persuaded you can say:

Well, I suppose you've got a point.
That's true.
I guess so.
Well, ok, but I need to see proof.
I suppose so.
You're right.

Podcast conversation part 3

Juan: What happened? When did you find out? How is he?

Laura: Calm down, he's not going to die.

Juan: I have to go home right now.

Laura: Juan, I understand you're upset, but if you just listen.

Juan: Laura, this is my brother! I have to go and be with him.

Laura: Juan, I know you feel that way, but you need to think this through.

Juan: What do you mean?

Laura: Well, your mum said that he is OK. They've got him on a lot of medication and he will be sleeping for the next 2 weeks while the pain is bad.

Juan: That's awful. I need to go. I have to be with my family.

Laura: I understand that, but your mum wants you to stay here and live your dream.

Juan: If I hadn't spent all my time working to earn money for this trip I could have spent more time with Charlie and taught him to drive properly!

Laura: You couldn't have stopped the accident even if you had been in the car with him.

Juan: But I…

Laura: Look, if you went back to England, you would give up your dream trip to sit in a hospital and drink bad coffee. You wouldn't be able to help Charlie.

Juan: I suppose so. But if I was there I could help my mum!

Laura: I understand what you're saying, but your mum said she doesn't want two of her sons in the hospital; she is so happy you're here in Thailand and wants you to continue your trip, at least until Charlie wakes up.

Juan: But what if something happened and I wasn't there, I could never forgive myself!

Laura: OK, how about this? I promised your mum we would Skype her in a couple of hours and you can discuss it with her then.

Juan: I guess so.

Pronunciation

Notice how when Laura wants to convince Juan of her idea, she lets him finish speaking first, and is positive about it before she disagrees. Her voice is soft and friendly. This way Juan will listen to her instead of being defensive and arguing with her. Practise the conversation.

Coming to a consensus

When you need to come to a decision you can say:

So shall we say six o'clock?
How about we say we decorate the kitchen first, then the bathroom?
Are we all agreed on yellow?
Do you agree that we go ahead?
So that's settled, we leave tomorrow.
Why don't we agree that we'll do this first, and that later?
How about this? We use both ideas, but in different places.
Can we say that we've come to a decision?
Right, so we're agreed?

KEY TIP 'Let's agree to disagree, shall we?' means 'We will not reach an agreement so let's move on.'

Podcast conversation part 4

2 hours later

Juan: Mum I really want to come home.

Lorena: No, Juan, I think it's better that you stay there.

Juan: But mum, this is Charlie we're talking about.

Lorena: Look, how about this? We speak every day on Skype, and if there is any change in his condition I will tell you and we can book you on the first flight home.

Juan: But mum, I want to be there with you and the family.

Lorena: I know sweetie, but this trip is your dream. Charlie would hate to be the one who spoiled that if you came home. Don't you think it would be better to have some great stories to tell him when he wakes up?

Juan: I don't know mum…

Lorena: Look at it this way. Charlie will definitely be asleep for 2 more weeks the doctors said. He's not in any danger so why don't we agree that you will stay for 2 more weeks and then we'll reassess when he wakes up?

Juan: Are you sure that's for the best?

Lorena: Absolutely. You have to consider that if you came home, Charlie would feel bad not only because of his injuries, but also because he had ruined your trip.

Juan: Well, I suppose that's true. I know he was very excited for me.

Lorena: Exactly, so are we agreed? You stay for another 2 weeks and we speak every day?

Juan: OK, but you have to promise me you'll tell me if there is any change at all.

Lorena: Deal. Now go and have some fun. Laura said something about tigers…

Time to Talk

1. Listen to all four parts of the podcast conversation between Laura, Juan and Lorena at www.learnenglish.education. Notice their pronunciation then practise reading the dialogues. Record yourself on your phone then listen back. Do you sound like the speakers?
2. Use Siri/Cortana/voice recognition software to check your pronunciation of the vocabulary. If the voice recognition software can understand you, you are doing well!

Remember, the more you practise, the better you will be.

Grammar

G13 The conditional tenses

Conditional sentences are made up of two clauses; the condition and the result. They can be used in these two ways:

	Condition	**Result**
1st	*If + subject + present* If he takes the car,	*subject + will + infinitive* he'll get there faster.
2nd	*If + subject + simple past* If I stopped eating chocolate,	*subject + would/could/might + infinitive* I would lose a few kilos.
3rd	*If + subject + past perfect* If you had studied more,	*subject + would/could/might have + infinitive* you would have passed the exam.

	Result	**Condition**
1st	*Subject + will + infinitive* He'll get there faster	*if + subject + present* if he takes the car.
2nd	*Subject + would/could/might + infinitive* I would lose a few kilos	*if + subject + past* if I stopped eating chocolate.
3rd	*Subject + would/could/might have + infinitive* You would have passed the exam	*if + subject + past perfect* if you had studied more.

10 In the news

Talking about current affairs

To tell someone about a news story you have read/seen/heard about you can say:

Have you read about the President's new plan?
Did you hear about the new shopping centre?
Did you see the news last night?
What do you think about the problems in the Middle East?
What's your take on the China deal?

To give information about what you have heard/read you can say:

According to the paper, unemployment is at an all-time high.
I heard that it was the worst storm in a decade.
From what I heard, it sounded like it was more serious than we thought.
They said on the news **that** there's going to be a riot.

Podcast conversation part 1

Oscar: So what do you think about the robbery?

Darrell: Robbery? What robbery?

Oscar: Didn't you see the news last night?

Darrell: No, I was working late, why? What's happened?

Oscar: They said on the news that yesterday someone broke into the National Gallery and stole three of the most valuable paintings. That's what they've discovered so far anyway; it might be more.

Darrell: Really? How did they manage that?

Oscar: I'm not sure, but according to the paper I read this morning, they think that there were at least two people involved, probably more, and a lot of careful planning.

Darrell: I can imagine. Do they know how they got in?

Oscar: From what I heard, it sounded like they were con artists rather than 'smash and grab' thieves, so the whole thing was really well planned, but the police are still investigating.

Darrell: Wow. Don't get me wrong, it's not that I support theft, but you have to admire the planning involved in doing something like this!

Oscar: I agree. It takes a lot of work to pull something like this off and not get caught!

Pronunciation

Listen to the conversation above, and focus on how Oscar pronounces the 'buffer phrases' ('well, apparently'; 'from what I heard...') then practise reading each part aloud and record yourself on your phone. Practise using the 'buffer phrases' and add your own news.

Being objective

When you are not sure if your information is accurate you can say:

They think that she was killed by her dog.
Some people think it's a conspiracy.
They believe it was his mother.
Well, apparently there's going to be a vote about it next year.
They're saying that he might be convicted of murder.
I don't know if it's true, but I heard there's going to be an investigation.

More formally you could say:

It seems that we weren't the only country involved.
It looks like there may be a war.
It appears that they were wrong.
It's been reported that they stole the money over a period of months.
It's been claimed that he took drugs to make himself run faster.
It's thought that £10 million was taken.

Grammar
See G14 on passive phrases on page 94.

Podcast conversation part 2

Darrell:	Hey, Oscar, have you heard the latest about the robbery?
Oscar:	No, why? What's happened?
Darrell:	Well, according to the news, a total of ten paintings were stolen!
Oscar:	Wow! Ten? That's a good haul for the thieves!
Darrell:	I know right? But guess how much they're worth.
Oscar:	No idea. A couple of million?
Darrell:	More! They say the total when they're sold will be about £130 million!
Oscar:	Sure, but it's not easy to sell paintings that famous, especially when they're being searched for by Interpol.
Darrell:	True, but it looks like these guys really know what they're doing. The buyers were probably lined up before they even went into the gallery.
Oscar:	So they think it was done to order?
Darrell:	Probably. I heard that Interpol is working with the police on this as well as the FBI.
Oscar:	I suppose their usual suspects are being investigated.
Darrell:	I should imagine so. They're going to have to work quickly if they want to catch these guys!
Oscar:	Yeah. I bet they're already out of the country!

Pronunciation

Practise the conversation reading both parts. Record yourself to see if you sound like Darrell and Oscar.

Improve your vocabulary: *check these new words using your dictionary app*

Crime	Criminal
murder	murderer
kidnapping	kidnapper
rape	rapist
robbery	robber
burglary	burglar
mugging	mugger
pickpocketing	pickpocket
shoplifting	shoplifter
fraud	con artist
drug trafficking	drug trafficker
dealing drugs	drug dealer
terrorism	terrorist
arson	arsonist
theft	thief
	ringleader
	mastermind
	snitch/grass/informant/source

Podcast conversation part 3

Oscar: Darrell, did you read the reports online, about how the police think those paintings were stolen?

Darrell: No. I haven't read anything yet. What do they think happened?

Oscar: Well, they've got a theory that the paintings weren't all taken in one night, but that they had been taken over a period of time and nobody noticed back then because they'd been replaced by really good fakes. Whoever the ringleader is, he has some great contacts, including a talented art forger.

Darrell: What?

Oscar: Yeah, they think that the criminals had been entering the gallery about once a week for the past few months and replacing the paintings.

Darrell: How did they find out?

Oscar:	From what I've read, it seems like one of the IT guys spotted a programming error in the security system.
Darrell:	Oh yeah?
Oscar:	Yeah. Whoever planned all this is a real criminal mastermind. It looks like a bug was created to crash the security for a couple of hours each week; long enough for someone to get in and switch the paintings.
Darrell:	That's amazing. And they say this had been going on for a couple of months before anyone noticed?
Oscar:	That's what I read. But now they're worried that this is part of a bigger thing and that other museums may have been hit in the same way!
Darrell:	Unbelievable! So now all the big museums and galleries are going to have to check their stock?
Oscar:	It looks that way. This could have been going on for years all over the world, undetected!
Darrell:	Wow!

Pronunciation

Listen to the conversation and read the script. Read both Darrell and Oscar's parts and record yourself on your phone. Listen back.

Grammar
See G15 on past perfect verbs on page 95.

Telling a story

KEY TIP

When we are telling a story in English, we usually use continuous tenses to describe actions that were happening in the background, and simple tenses to describe the actions that are our focus, e.g.:

It was a beautiful morning; the sun was shining, the birds were singing and I was walking to the bakery to buy my breakfast when I saw a man run out of the jewellery shop!

When setting the scene you can say:

It was a normal Monday evening.
The neighbours **were** shout**ing and the** dog **was** bark**ing**.
I hadn't been home long **and I was** cook**ing** dinner.
I'd been planning to order pizza **but then I remembered** I had no money.
I was about to turn on the oven, **when** there was a power cut.

When introducing a surprise you can say:

Suddenly I heard a bang.
All of a sudden it got very dark.
Just at that moment the phone rang.
Just as I sent the e-mail, there was a message on my screen.
Out of nowhere came a loud scream.
Out of the blue there was a knock at the door.

To give more information, talk about your reactions you can say:

I was totally terrified/furious/speechless.
It was really unexpected/weird/strange/odd.
I didn't know what was going on.
I had no idea what do to.
I felt utterly helpless/pretty silly/rather ashamed/completely lost.
I'd never been so scared/happy/embarrassed.

To make comments about the story you can say:

The funny thing was, I didn't know her name.
You'll never believe it, but he let me in for free.
You can imagine how shocked I was.
Honestly, it was the most incredible thing.
I know how this sounds, but I swear it's true!
You've never seen anything like it; everyone was just standing there, looking up at nothing.
I never thought I'd say this, but Justin Bieber was brilliant!
And the craziest part of all was that they thought I was an actress!

Podcast conversation part 4

Oscar: Hey man, so what's your take on this art thief conspiracy? Do you actually believe it?

Darrell: Well, you never know. I was reading a really interesting interview with one of the gallery guards online yesterday. Hang on, I'll find it and read it to you.

Oscar: I dunno, it all sounds a bit crazy to me.

Darrell: Here it is. OK so he said,... hang on, I'm gonna read it to you.

Oscar: OK.

Darrell: 'It was a typical Saturday night about 6 months ago. I always work the night shift and I was doing my first round of the gallery, where we have to check there's nobody in there, when suddenly I heard a noise coming from upstairs. I got my torch and baton and walked to the stairwell. I was about to go up the stairs when I heard a bang from the room I'd just left. At this point I was getting really nervous so I decided to call the other guard, but he was in the bathroom, so I thought I'd go upstairs and investigate there. When I got into the main gallery it looked empty, but at the end of the hall there was a painting missing. I was taking out my Walkie Talkie to call the police, when the gallery curator came out from behind a sculpture and told me that he'd had the painting taken for repair and it would be back by Monday morning. Well, I know how this sounds in light of what we now know, but at the time it seemed reasonable, as some of the paintings had been damaged in the past, so I believed him and went back downstairs.'

Oscar: So based on that they think that it was an inside job and the gallery curator was responsible?

Darrell: Yeah. They're now going to investigate all of the places this guy had worked before and see if any other works are missing. If so, then he and his conspirators are going away for a long time.

Oscar: Do they have any proof?

Darrell: I don't know. This guy has only just come forward, so I guess there's a lot of investigating to do to get to the bottom of it all.

Oscar: Well good luck to them!

Pronunciation

Remember, when you tell a story, use your voice to help create the atmosphere. Listen to the conversation and how Darrell reads the guard's story. The music of his voice helps us to understand the story.

Time to Talk

1. Listen to all four parts of the conversation between Oscar and Darrell at www.learnenglish2.education. Notice their pronunciation then practise reading the dialogues. Record yourself on your phone then listen back. Do you sound like the speakers?
2. Use Siri/Cortana/voice recognition software to check your pronunciation of the vocabulary. If the voice recognition software can understand you, you are doing well!

Remember, the more you practise, the better you will be.

Grammar

G14 The passive

When we want to talk about an action but we are not sure who did it, or that information is not important, we use the phrases described above on page 88 and we often the passive voice. We also use it when we don't want to accuse somebody directly of an action. Consider the phrases below:

Active	Passive
The police usually catch criminals.	Criminals are usually caught (by the police).
The police are investigating the crime.	The crime is being investigated (by the police).
The police arrested the robber.	The robber was arrested (by the police).
The police were chasing the gang members.	The gang members were being chased (by the police).
The police have sealed off the area.	The area has been sealed off (by the police).
The police have been watching Carl for a while.	Carl has been watched for a while (by the police).
The police had identified the kidnapper.	The kidnapper had been identified (by the police).

The police had been recording Joe's calls for weeks.	Joe's calls had been recorded for weeks (by the police).
The police are going to interrogate the suspect.	The suspect is going to be interrogated (by the police).
The police will recover the stolen goods.	The stolen goods will be recovered (by the police).

To form the passive we use: subject + *be* + V3 (+ by). The object of the action becomes the subject of the sentence, the verb *be* takes the tense and the action is in V3. It is not always necessary to say who does the action.

For more information see the ***Grammar guide*** *on pages 119–128.*

G15 The past perfect simple and continuous

Look at podcast conversation part 3. Notice how when we talk about an event that happened BEFORE a time in the past, we use the past perfect:

Past perfect simple: subject + had + V3 e.g. *they had been taken.*
Past perfect continuous: subject + had been + V-ing, e.g. *the criminals had been entering.*

Look at the examples in conversation 3; both of these events happened **before** anybody noticed the crime. This is why we use the past perfect.

For more information see the ***Grammar guide*** *on pages 119–128.*

11 Holidays

At your accommodation

If you haven't booked a room (or if you are booking over the phone) you can say:

Hello/Good morning/afternoon/evening,

do you have any double rooms available for 2 nights?

do you have any vacancies?

I'm looking for a single room for 4 nights.

I'm hoping you have a dorm bed for tonight.

I'd like an en-suite, twin room for 5 nights if you have one available?

is there any chance I could book a double room with sea view for the next 3 nights?

When you arrive at a place you have booked you can say:

Hello/Good morning/afternoon/evening,

my name's Joy Moore and **I have a reservation for** the honeymoon suite.

I'd like to check in, please.

I've got a reservation for a single room for 2 nights.

I've got a room booked in the name of Filipo Borlotti.

Brenda Roberts. **I've booked a room for** 3 nights.

If you want more information you can ask:

Could I get a wake-up call at 7.30 a.m., please?
What time is breakfast/lunch/dinner **served?**
Would it be possible to have a late check out?
Do you have a left luggage facility/gym/swimming pool/gift shop?
Could you tell me where the nearest cashpoint/bank/metro stop is?
Could you recommend a local restaurant/museum/park?
Where should I leave my suitcase/go for breakfast?

If there is a problem with your room and you call reception you can say:

I'm sorry but there seems to be no heating in my room.
There doesn't appear to be a remote control for the TV.
I'm afraid my room is too noisy. **Would it be possible to change to another one?**
Sorry to be a pain, but the fridge in my room isn't working properly.
Sorry, but it looks like housekeeping forgot to replace my towels.
I wonder if you can help me. I'd like an extra pillow **please.**
I'm sorry, I booked a sea view **and this room is** garden view.

Podcast conversation part 1

Istvan: Good afternoon. How can I help you?

Dawn: Oh. Good Afternoon. Er. My name's Dawn Lakeside and I have a reservation for two nights.

Istvan: Of course madam, a double room en-suite with a garden view, is that right?

Dawn: Yes, that sounds about right.

Istvan: Here's your key-card and you're in room 317 on the third floor. The elevator is just over there.

Dawn: Oh, thank you, but I'll take the stairs. What time is breakfast served?

Istvan: Between 7 and 10 in the restaurant. It's usually busiest at around 8.

Dawn: Good to know, thank you.

Phone rings

Istvan:	Good afternoon, reception.
Dawn:	Hello again, it's Ms Lakeside in room 317. There seems to be a problem with my TV. Could you get somebody to look at it for me please?
Istvan:	Oh, sorry about that madam. I'll send somebody up right away.
Dawn:	Thank you.
Istvan:	Is that everything?
Dawn:	Actually no. Sorry to be a pain, but it looks like housekeeping forgot to put towels in the bathroom.
Istvan:	I'm so sorry, It's been a very busy day for housekeeping. I'll send some to you right away. Anything else?
Dawn:	No, thank you.
Istvan:	Enjoy your evening Ms Lakeside.
Dawn:	I will, thank you.

Pronunciation

Listen to the conversation above, then practise reading each part aloud and record yourself on your phone. Practise Dawn's part of the conversation but with different problems.

Improve your vocabulary: *check any new words using your dictionary app*

Types of holiday
Go on a/an:
beach holiday/getaway
walking/sailing/diving/skiing holiday
cruise
yoga retreat
adventure holiday
mini-break/city-break/short break
Join an **organised tour**
Go **camping/backpacking/travelling**

Types of accommodation
hotel
guest house
B&B (Bed and Breakfast)
campsite
hostel
holiday cottage/home/apartment
yacht
hotel

Types of room
single room
double room
twin room
triple room
dormitory
en-suite
room with balcony/terrace
room with sea/garden/mountain view

Reporting what someone said

We often tell people what somebody has said to us. This is known as 'reported speech' and to do it, we change the grammar in a few ways.

Grammar
See G16 on reported speech on page 105.

To tell someone what somebody else has said you can say:

Direct: 'I'm meeting her tomorrow.'
Reported: **She said** she was meeting her **the next day/the day after.**

Direct: 'I did it yesterday.'
Reported: **He told me** he'd done it **the previous day/the day before.**

Direct: 'I saw it **this morning.**'
Reported: **She explained to me that** she'd seen it **that morning.**

Direct: 'The food was terrible, but we ate it.'
Reported: **He claimed that** the food was terrible, but I'm not sure because they ate it!

Direct: 'We can go to the shop on the way home if you like.'
Reported: **She suggested we could go to the shop on the way home.**

Podcast conversation part 2

On the phone

Dawn: Hey! Yeah, I got here safely. The hotel seems nice apart from a couple of problems in my room.

Gemma: Oh no! What was wrong?

Dawn: Well, the TV wasn't tuned in and there were no towels when I arrived.

Gemma: That's not good. What did you do?

Dawn: I called the guy at reception and asked him to sort it out.

Gemma: And?

Dawn: Well the guy said that he was sending someone up, but I waited another 20 minutes for them to get here.

Gemma: Well, at least it's sorted out now. So, I'm arriving tomorrow morning. Can you organise a taxi for me from the airport? My plane lands at ten and I haven't got any checked luggage.

Dawn: Of course. I'll call reception now. See you tomorrow!

Gemma: See you!

Improve your vocabulary: *check any new words using your dictionary app*

Reporting verbs		
say (said) tell (told) ask explain claim	whispered insist suggest mention promise	demand argue (argued) report
For more reporting verbs, go to http://www.ef.com/english-resources/english-grammar/reporting-verbs/		

KEY TIP

People often confuse **say** and **tell**. To help you remember, say means to speak the words, but tell means to pass information to another person. In many situations we can use both, but when specific information is given directly to another person, we use 'tell', and when general information is given to anybody who wants to listen, we use 'say', e.g.:

The weather forecaster said it would be nice today.

The teacher told me to do my homework again.

When we use 'tell' we must use a direct object – 'he told me' not 'he told'.

Podcast conversation part 3

Phone rings

Istvan: Hello, reception. How can I help?

Dawn: Hello again, it's Ms Lakeside. I was wondering if you could book a taxi to the hotel for my friend.

Istvan: Of course. Where from and what time?

Dawn: She's coming from the airport and she said that her plane lands at ten.

Istvan: So what time do you think the taxi should meet her?

Dawn: Well, she told me she hasn't got any checked luggage so maybe half past ten?

Istvan: Of course, and what's her name?

Dawn: It's Gemma Trent.

Istvan: No problem Ms Lakeside. The driver will be waiting for her at arrivals.

Dawn: Thank you.

Pronunciation

Listen to the conversation and read the script. Read both Dawn and Istvan's parts and record yourself on your phone. Listen back.

Talking about the weather

When talking about what the weather is doing now you can say:

It's really humid **at the moment.**
It's just so muggy **today.**
It's such a beautiful **day.**
It's blowing a gale **out there.**
It's absolutely freezing **today.**
I can't believe how chilly **it's got.**
What a lovely **day! Clear blue skies and sunshine.**
It's perfect kite-flying **weather!**

To talk about the weather in the past or future you can say:

They say it's going to be hot tomorrow, although I rarely believe the weather forecast.
Apparently there are going to be hailstorms at the weekend.
They say it'll turn cold **at the weekend.**
I bet we'll have an Indian Summer this year.
It looks like it's going to be a nice afternoon.
Last summer was a complete washout; it rained every single day!
It's typical April **weather.**

To talk about your weather preferences you can say:

I'm not a big fan of tropical climates.
I don't do cold.
I really hate the winter
I can't bear the heat.
I'm a warm weather person.

Podcast conversation part 4

Gemma: I can't believe I've got to go shopping for clothes!

Dawn: Why do you need more clothes?

Gemma: Well, on the weather forecast they said it was going to be cool and windy, but it's scorching out there! I've brought clothes for chilly weather.

Dawn: Haha, that'll teach you for trusting the weather forecast!

Gemma: I know. You told me it was going to be beautiful, with blue skies and sunshine. I can't believe how warm it is. It's only March!

Dawn: You know me, I'm a warm weather girl; I wouldn't have come here if it was going to be miserable and grey!

Gemma: That's true. You promised it wouldn't be cold. I wish I'd listened!

Dawn: Well you should buy enough for the whole week because it looks like it's going to stay hot!

Time to Talk

1. Listen to all four parts of the podcast conversation between Dawn, Istvan and Gemma at www.learnenglish2.education. Notice their pronunciation then practise reading the dialogues. Record yourself on your phone then listen back. Do you sound like the speakers?
2. Use Siri/Cortana/voice recognition software to check your pronunciation of the vocabulary. If the voice recognition software can understand you, you are doing well!

Remember, the more you practise, the better you will be.

Grammar

G16 Reported speech

Tense change

We usually **change the tense** when we report speech, although it isn't always necessary. Look at the timeline:

5.00pm: Fred is talking to Lars: '**I'm** going home.'
6.00pm: Lars is talking to Janet: 'Fred said he **was** going home.'

Lars uses the past continuous, because Fred's statement is now in the past.

The tenses usually change as shown in the table below

Direct speech *Fred to Lars*	**Reported speech** *Lars telling Janet what Fred said*
Present simple *'I don't watch TV much.'*	Past simple *'Fred said he didn't watch TV much.'*
Present continuous *'I'm taking my medicine.'*	Past continuous *'Fred said he was taking his medicine.'*
Present perfect simple *'I've seen that film.'*	Past perfect simple *'Fred said he'd seen that film.'*
Present perfect continuous *'I've been fixing my car all afternoon.'*	Past perfect continuous *'Fred said he'd been fixing his car all afternoon.'*
Past simple *'I cooked dinner last night.'*	Past perfect simple *'Fred said he'd cooked dinner last night.'*
Past continuous *'I was reading all night.'*	Past perfect continuous *'Fred said he'd been reading all night.'*
Past perfect simple *'I'd already eaten when they arrived.'*	Past perfect simple *'Fred said he'd already eaten when they arrived.'*
Past perfect continuous *'I'd been studying for ages.'*	Past perfect continuous *'Fred said he'd been studying for ages.'*

Changing the tense **isn't always necessary**, especially if you are in the same time period, e.g. this week/this month. Consider:

Fred: *'I haven't been to work this week because I'm so ill.'*

Lars to Janet: *'Fred said he* ***hasn't been*** *to work this week because he'****s*** *so ill.'*

We use the **same tense** because it's the **same time period**. We are still in 'this week'.

But

Lars to Janet: *'Fred told me he* ***hadn't been*** *to work because he* ***was*** *so ill.'*

This **changes** because the week **Fred was talking about** is now **in the past**.

We don't change tense either when we describe **facts or habits**, e.g.

Fred: *'I love pizza.'* Lars: *'Fred said he loves pizza.'*

We use the **same tense** because it is **still true**. Fred *always* loves pizza.

Personal pronouns

We **change some personal pronouns** to keep the same meaning:

Fred: *'****I*** *took* ***my*** *brother to the airport.'*
Lars: *'Fred said* ***he*** *took* ***his*** *brother to the airport.'*

Fred: *'Lars, Ute borrowed* ***your*** *book for* ***her*** *project.'*

Lars: *'Fred said Ute had borrowed* ***my*** *book for* ***her*** *project.'*

Fred: *'It took* **us** *3 hours to get home!'*

Lars: *'Fred said it had taken* ***them*** *3 hours to get home.'*

Time phrases

We **change some time phrases** to keep the same meaning:

Fred (**on Monday**): *'I watched TV all day* ***yesterday****.'*

Lars (**on Tuesday**): *'Fred said he had watched TV all day* ***on Sunday****.'*

Fred (**in 2015**): *'I got married* ***last year****.'*

Lars (**in 2016**): *'Fred said he got married* ***2 years ago****.'*

Fred **(on Saturday)**: *'I'm meeting Ravi tomorrow.'*

Lars **(later on Saturday)**: *'Fred said he's meeting Ravi tomorrow.'*

We don't change here because tomorrow has the same meaning.

Place references

We **change some place references** to keep the same meaning:

Fred (**in London**): *'I live 20 minutes* ***from here****.'*

Lars (**in Oxford**): *'Fred said he lives 20 minutes* ***from London/from there****.'*

Fred (**in Chicago**): *'Gothenburg is a great city, I really want to* ***go there****.'*

Lars (**in Gothenburg**): *'Fred said Gothenburg is a great city, he really wants to* ***come here****.'*

Reporting verbs

We **use a reporting verb** to introduce the reported speech:

Fred: *'Sorry I'm late Lars, I've been stuck in traffic.'*

Lars to Janet: *'Fred* ***explained*** *he was late because he'd been stuck in traffic.'*

Reporting questions

Closed questions

In addition to changing tenses/times/pronouns for closed questions we use **if/whether**, and change the question to statement form:

Fred: *'Lars, do you like pizza?'*

Lars to Janet: *'Fred* ***asked me*** *if I liked pizza.'*

Open questions

For open questions, we use **the question word** and change the question to a statement:

Fred: *'Why aren't you coming to Spain?'*

Lars to Janet: *'Fred* ***asked me*** *why I wasn't going to Spain.'*

Fred: *'When will you arrive in Beijing?'*

Lars to Janet: *'Fred* ***asked me*** *when I would arrive in Beijing.'*

Reporting instructions

To report instructions use the infinitive with to:

Fred: *'Close the door when you leave.'*

Lars to Janet: *'Fred* ***told us*** *to close the door when we left.'*

12 The future

Talking about future plans

To find out about somebody's future plans you can ask:

Where do you see yourself in 5 years' time?
What are your plans for the summer?
What will you be doing this time next year?
What do you plan to do when your contract finishes here?
Do you have any plans for New Year?
What's your dream?

To tell someone about your plans for the future, which have already been arranged you can say:

I'm having lunch with Dana next Tuesday.
The plan is to meet at the airport.

For things you have already decided but not arranged you can say:

I'm going to buy a new handbag.
I'm hoping to get a new job after the summer.
We're planning to build an extension.
We're looking to expand our company.
We intend to move early next year.

When you have just decided what to do you can say:

I'll probably go to Tenerife.
I'm not sure, **I should imagine I'll** take a taxi.
I think I'll have the Portobello Burger, what about you?

Podcast conversation part 1

Helen: Hi, good to see you! I can't believe it's been 6 months!

Vic: I know! The time has flown. So how are you?

Helen: Yeah, I'm fine thanks, just busy making plans.

Vic: Oh? Anything I should know about?

Helen:	Actually yeah, that's kinds why I asked you here for lunch. Pat and I have made a decision.
Vic:	Oh?
Helen:	Yeah, we've decided to move to Canada after the wedding.
Vic:	Really? Wow that's amazing. When are you going to go?
Helen:	Well, nothing is set in stone yet, but we're hoping to start working on my visa application after we're married.
Vic:	OK. Tell me more.
Helen:	Well, we're meeting with the immigration officer at the embassy on Friday to find out exactly what we have to do – well, what I have to do, Pat's Canadian.
Vic:	Right. Sure.
Helen:	They need nurses in Canada so the plan is to get my visa, and then retrain for Canadian nursing when I get there.
Vic:	And what about location?
Helen:	Well, we'd like to be near Pat's family, but not too close!
Vic:	Haha, I can understand that. Families are great, but not all the time!
Helen:	Exactly, so we're planning to move either to Toronto or Montreal.
Vic:	Wow! Well, I think this calls for some celebratory champagne!

Pronunciation

Listen to the conversation above, and then practise reading each part aloud and record yourself on your phone.

Talking about future situations

Grammar

See G17 on the future perfect and the future continuous on page 116.

To describe your life in the future you can say:

By the time I'm 35 **I will have** visited 36 countries.
By October next year, **he'll have been** working for that company for 6 years.
I'll be an expert **by then.**

This time next year **I'll have** finished my degree.
In 5 weeks' **time, I'll be** start**ing** my new job.
If everything goes according to plan, they'll be study**ing** here in a year or two.
When I eventually finish the project, **I'll have been** liv**ing** in Malaysia for 3 years.

I should imagine I'll still be working for the bank.
I suppose I will have got my driving licence.
I'll probably be relaxing on a beach somewhere.
I'll most likely have started my own business.

Podcast conversation part 2

A few months later

Vic:	Hi Helen. How was the honeymoon?
Helen:	Excellent, thanks.
Vic:	So, how are the plans for Canada coming along?
Helen:	Really well, thanks. With any luck, this time next year we'll be moving there!
Vic:	Wow, so soon?
Helen:	Yeah, we want to go as soon as possible. By that time Pat will have been living abroad for 10 years and he's really looking forward to going back home.
Vic:	I can imagine. What about you? What will you be doing?
Helen:	Well, I'll be busy settling us into our new home and enrolling on the nursing transfer course.
Vic:	And what about Pat?
Helen:	Well, he'll be starting his new job as soon as we arrive.
Vic:	That's great. Well, in that case, I'd better start looking at flights to come and visit!
Helen:	Absolutely! You should come for Christmas. We'll have settled in by then and we'll be able to show you the best places in the city.
Vic:	Sounds great. I'll need a break as I'll most likely still be at the same job!

Pronunciation

Practise the conversation reading both parts. Record yourself to see if you sound like Vic and Helen, then describe your life in 5 years time; what will you be doing? What about this time next year? What about Sunday afternoon?

Making comparisons

When you want to make direct comparisons between things you can say:

Gay marriage **is much more common than** it was 5 years ago.
Finland is **far colder than** Spain.
Sweden **isn't as** pretty **as** Italy, **but it's a lot more** efficient.
I've noticed it's **rather more expensive** to buy food in Norway **than** in Brazil.
South Africa **is as** beautiful **as** New Zealand.

KEY TIP Notice how we use **than**, or **as**, when comparing two different things.

When you want to talk about things changing over a period of time, you can say:

It's becoming more and more difficult to find a job.
It's going to get increasingly harder to buy your own house.
Educational standards **have got higher and higher** in Africa over the last 20 years.
I expect it'll be **a lot more attractive** to move abroad if this tax law is passed.
It's becoming far easier to communicate with all the new apps available.
Our summers are **rather hotter** than they used to be.
Human Rights are becoming **much more** important.

Grammar
See G18 on short and long adjectives on page 117.

When you want to talk about the consequences of changes you can say:

We can agree that **the more** we fight, **the** angrier we get.
I'd say **the bigger, the better.**
I've discovered that **the harder** I try, **the more likely** I am to pass the exam.
Well, **the more** hours I work, **the less** time I have to spend money!
Unfortunately, **the more** I exercise, **the more** I eat!
On the bright side, **the fewer** people that come to the party, **the less** cleaning up there will be.

KEY TIP Many idioms take this form, e.g.
'The bigger they are, the harder they fall.'
'The more the merrier'.
'The bigger the better'.

Podcast conversation part 3

Phone rings

Helen: Hello?

Vic: Hey Helen, how's it going in Canada?

Helen: Vic! So good to hear from you! Yeah, every day it's getting better and better.

Vic: I'm so glad to hear it. So I saw on Facebook that you're starting work next month?

Helen: Yep. This time next week I'll have finished the diploma and I'll be working in the local hospital.

Vic: That's fantastic. So, what about my visit?

Helen: Haha, I was hoping you'd say that. The closer we get to Christmas, the higher the prices of the flights, so I'd recommend booking soon!

Vic: OK. Yeah, I'd noticed that they're rather more expensive in December than they were in April.

Helen: Yeah, you know how it is, the more popular the flight, the higher the price, and unfortunately for you, Christmas is a popular time to come to Canada.

Vic: I should imagine it is. So how are you finding living there rather than just visiting?

Helen: It's great. I'm meeting more and more people every week and that'll increase again when I start work. Pat's also made lots of friends so our social life is really good.

Vic: Cool, and what about practicalities, like finding a place to live?

Helen: Yeah, it took a couple of weeks, but now we have a gorgeous apartment right by the park, and rent is far cheaper here per square metre than in London. I can't wait for you to see it.

Vic:	Nor can I! Well, I'll have a look at dates and get back to you next week if that's OK?
Helen:	Sure, although I'll be working from Wednesday, so better to call me before then if you can.
Vic:	No worries.

Pronunciation

Listen to the conversation and read the script. Read both Vic and Helen's parts and record yourself on your phone. Listen back.

Talking about dreams and aspirations

When you want to talk about future dreams that you don't think will happen you can say:

I wish I could move to San Francisco.
If only I could quit my job and travel forever.
It would be amazing if I could retrain as a lawyer.
My dream is to learn Japanese.
I dream of one day opening an animal sanctuary.
One of these days I'm going to be rich.
I've always wanted to know how planes actually fly.
It'll never happen, but I'd like to be an actress.
My fantasy is to win the lottery and spend the rest of my life reading books.
Wouldn't it be amazing if I became President?

When you think they may happen, but you're not sure when, you can say:

I'd love to go to the Caribbean.
I'd like to be an actress.
I really want to see that play.
One day I'll actually clear out my wardrobe.
At some point, I'm going to decorate the bathroom.
I really ought to buy a new car **soon.**

Podcast conversation part 4

Vic:	Hi Chloe! How are you?
Chloe:	Really well thanks. What about you? How was your trip to Canada?
Vic:	It was awesome! The best week I've had all year.
Chloe:	That's great! How are Helen and Pat doing?
Vic:	Great! They're living the dream. I wish I could just up and leave and start again somewhere warm and sunny!
Chloe:	Yeah, me too. I've always wanted to open a little café in the countryside.
Vic:	I can imagine you doing that!
Chloe:	Yeah, yeah, one day maybe. What about you? What do you dream of doing?
Vic:	To be honest I'm not sure. I mean, of course it would be amazing if I could move to somewhere like Brazil and spend my life relaxing on a beach, maybe run a little beach bar and just enjoy the pace of life…
Chloe:	Ha! Never, you're too much of a Londoner! You'd go crazy if you spent more than a couple of months away from this city!
Vic:	That's true. In that case, I'd love to get a better job here so I could work from home 4 days a week and have 3 day weekends every week, not to mention 2 months paid holiday of course!
Chloe:	Sounds to me like you need to start your own business!
Vic:	Now there's an idea…

Pronunciation

Now you have come to the end of the book, listen to all of the podcast conversations again. Notice the language, use of voice and intonation and practise recording yourself repeating all of them. Remember, it is only by speaking, practising and playing with new language that it becomes natural, and you become both more confident and more fluent in your speaking.

Time to Talk

1. Listen to all four parts of the conversation between Vic, Helen and Chloe at www.learnenglish2.education. Notice their pronunciation then practise reading the dialogues. Record yourself on your phone then listen back. Do you sound like the speakers?
2. Use Siri/Cortana/voice recognition software to check your pronunciation of the vocabulary. If the voice recognition software can understand you, you are doing well!

Remember, the more you practise, the better you will be.

Grammar

G17 Future perfect and future continuous

When we want to describe our lives in the future we can use a variety of tenses. Consider:

A *By the time you* ***get*** *this letter,* ***I will have left*** *Singapore.*

B *When I finally* ***get*** *my qualification,* ***I will have been studying*** *engineering for 4 years.*

C *If everything* ***goes*** *according to plan, this time next year* ***I will be living*** *in Beijing.*

- **A is the future perfect** (**subject + will + have +V3**). It is used to talk about something that will finish **before** a time in the future. It is often used with 'by the time'.
- **B is the future perfect continuous** (**subject + will +have been + V-ing**). It is used to talk about something that will have been in progress for a period of time at a particular point in the future.
- **C is the future continuous (subject + will be + V-ing)**. It is used to describe something that will be in progress as part of normal life; not a special plan, more a background action.

Remember that we don't use **state** verbs in the continuous tenses, e.g. be, know, believe, like, love… For these verbs we use future simple (subject + will + V1).

For time lines check the ***Grammar guide*** *on pages 119–128.*

G18 Short and long adjectives for describing changes

Short adjectives	Long adjectives
hotter and hotter	more and more important
better and better	less and less interesting
increasingly bigger	increasingly more expensive
far shorter	far more/less suitable
a lot harder	a lot more/less exciting
much happier	much more/less entertaining
rather colder	rather more/less

Grammar guide

Tenses

Key:

X	*the action*
~	*the action in progress*
→	*the effect of the action*
D	*the decision to perform the action*
A	*the arrangement to take the action*

Present simple

When used:

- to describe habits and regular activities, e.g. daily routine.
- to describe permanent or long lasting situations e.g. opinions, feelings, job.
- to describe facts and timetables. (Can be used for a future meaning with timetables)

Timeline:

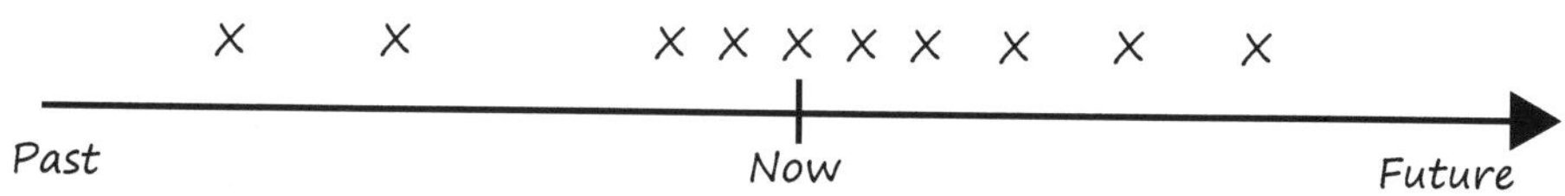

Structure
Positive: subject + V1 **but** in third person singular add an 's' to V1. e.g. she eats
Negative: subject + don't/doesn't + V1
Interrogative: [question word] + do/does + subject + V1

Examples:

I walk my dog every day
She doesn't like pizza!
Do they take credit cards?

Present continuous

When used:

- to talk about things happening now, at this moment
- to describe things happening around this time
- to talk about plans in the future that are definite and arranged

Timeline:

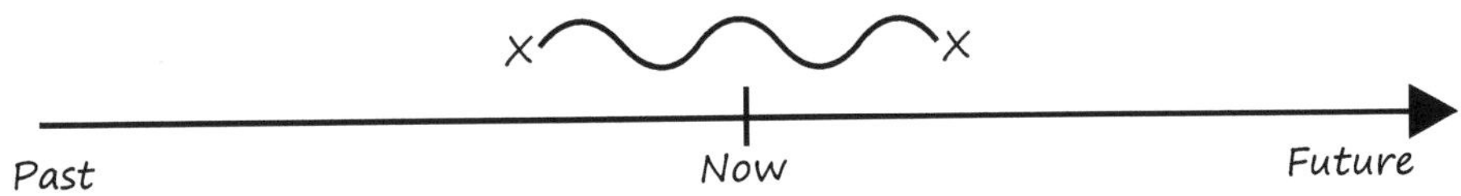

Structure
Positive: subject + be (conjugated) + V-ing
Negative: subject + be (conjugated) + not + V-ing
Interrogative: [question word] + be (conjugated) + subject + V-ing

Examples:

They're running a good campaign.
I'm not taking the English exam this summer.
What are you doing?

Past simple

When used:

- to talk about actions that have finished
- to describe actions that happened at a particular time
- to talk about facts in the past

Timeline:

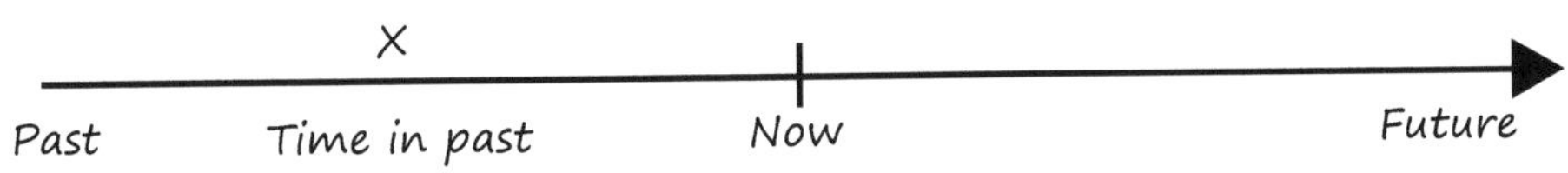

Structure
Positive: subject + V2
Negative: subject + didn't + V1
Interrogative: [question word] + did + subject + V1

Examples:

She walked to the shop.
You didn't eat your vegetables.
Did we bring enough money?

Past continuous

When used:

- to describe something that was happening at an exact moment in the past.
- to describe actions that were interrupted in the past (used with past simple)
- to describe background actions in the past

Timeline:

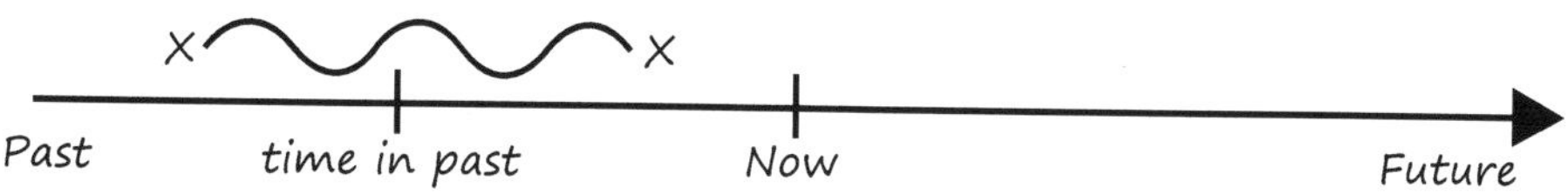

Structure

Positive: subject + was/were + V-ing
Negative: subject + wasn't/weren't + V-ing
Interrogative: [question word] + was/were + subject + V-ing

Examples:

I was watching TV last night.
He wasn't driving too fast officer!
Were you eating when I called?

Present perfect simple

When used:

- to describe something completed in the past that is still important now
- to talk about experience
- to talk about things that have happened and may happen again
- to focus on the result of an action, rather than the action itself
- to focus on the number of times something has happened (how many)

Timeline:

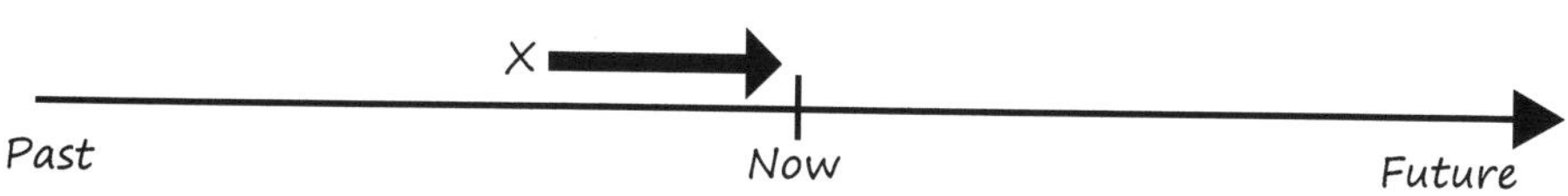

Structure

Positive: subject + have/has + V3
Negative: subject + haven't/hasn't +V3
Interrogative: [question word] + have/has + subject + [ever] + V3

Examples:

I've lost my keys.
Tom hasn't visited me this month.
Have you ever been to New York?

Present perfect continuous

When used:

- to talk about things that have started, but are unfinished/still happening
- to talk about something that was happening, but recently or just stopped
- to focus on the action rather than the result of the action
- to focus on the duration of an action (how long)

Timeline:

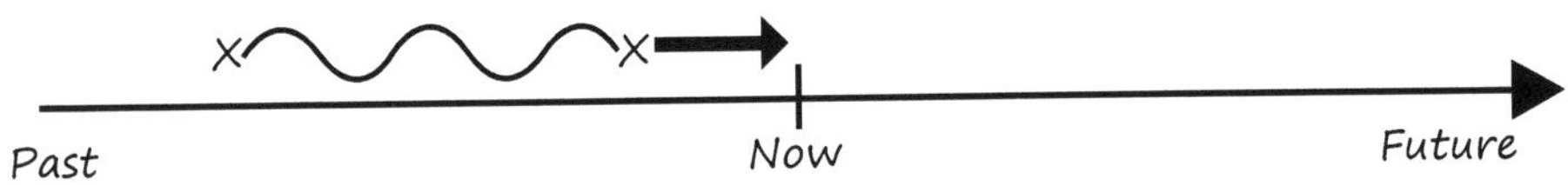

Positive: subject + have/has + been + V-ing
Negative: subject + haven't/hasn't + been + V-ing
Interrogative: [question word] + have/has + subject + been + V-ing

Examples:

I've been learning English for 6 years.
Grandma is ill because she hasn't been taking her medicine.
You look exhausted, have you been working all night?

Past perfect simple

When used:

- to describe something that happened before a specific time/event in the past.
- to describe experience you already had at a certain time in the past.

Timeline:

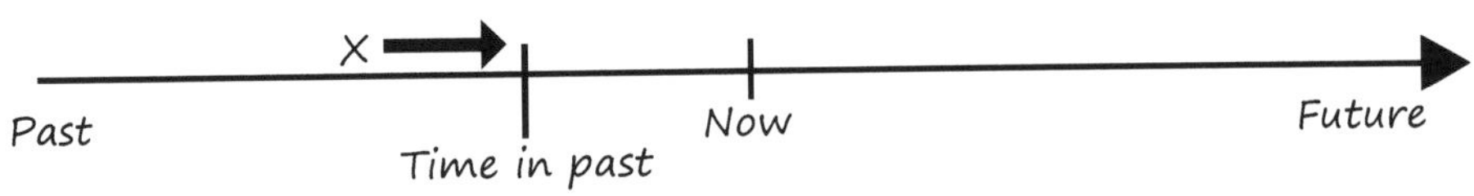

Positive: subject + had + V3
Negative: subject + hadn't + V3
Interrogative: (question word) + had + subject + V3

Examples:

I had taken my driving test 3 days before.
She hadn't flown before and this was her first holiday abroad.
Why didn't you go to the cinema with him? Had you already seen the film?

Past perfect continuous

When used:

- to talk about something that was happening for a period of time before something else happened in the past

Timeline:

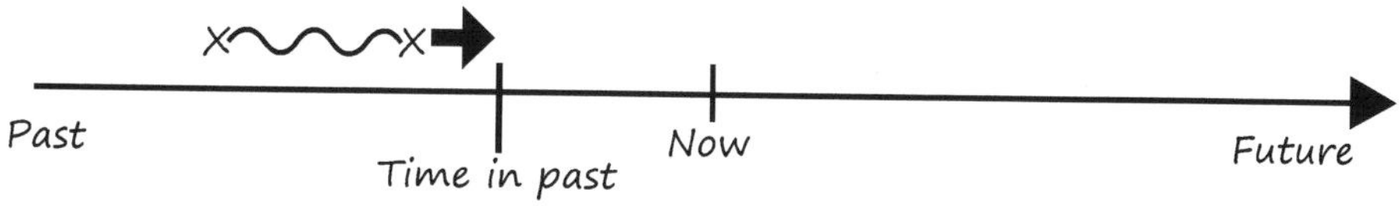

Positive: subject + had + been + V-ing
Negative: subject + hadn't + been +V-ing
Interrogative: [question word] + had + subject + been + V-ing

Examples:

When I went into her room last night it smelled awful. She had been smoking in there.
George went to the doctor last Monday. He hadn't been feeling well all weekend.
Had you been waiting long when the bus arrived?

Future simple

When used:

- for predictions
- for offers, promises and decisions just made
- for scheduled events

Timeline:

D = decision; A = arrangement; X = action. All three things happen with every action we do.

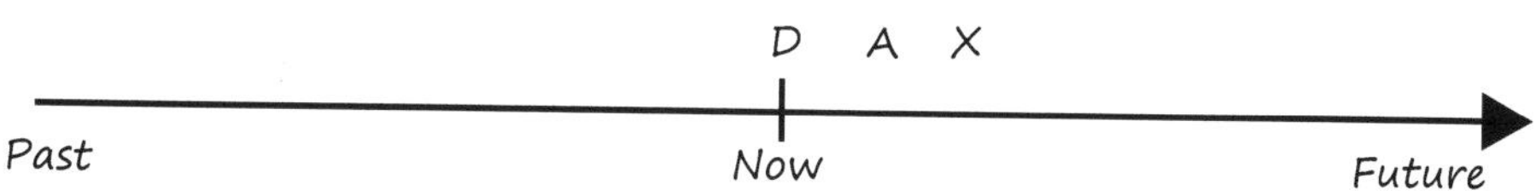

Positive: subject + will + V1
Negative: subject + won't + V1
Interrogative: [question word] + will + subject + V1

Examples:

I'll open the door.
He won't drive too fast.
Will you hold my bag please?

Future with 'going to'

When used:

- to express planned events or intentions, decided on *before* the moment of speaking
- for future predictions based on physical evidence
- for personal plans and schedules

Timeline:

D = decision; A = arrangement; X = action. All three things happen with every action we do.

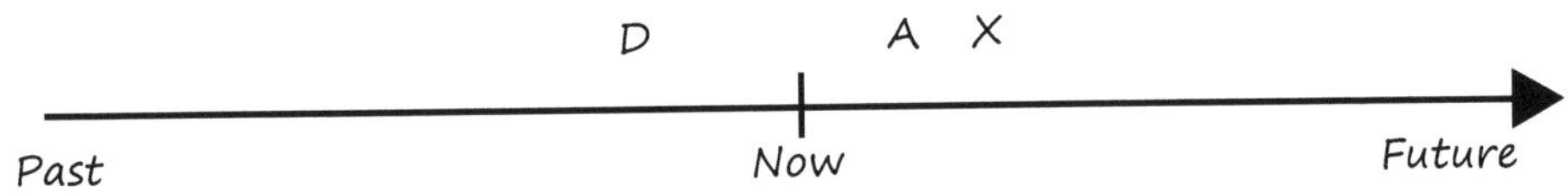

Positive: subject + be (conjugated) + going to + V1
Negative: subject + be (conjugated) + not going to + V1
Interrogative: [question word] + be (conjugated) + subject + going to + V1

Examples:

I'm going to play tennis tomorrow afternoon.
They're not going to have much time at the park if they stay in the pub any longer!
Where are you going to go on holiday?

Present continuous for future plans

When used:

- to talk about things happening now, at this moment
- to describe thing happening around this time
- to talk about plans in the future that are definite and arranged

Timeline:

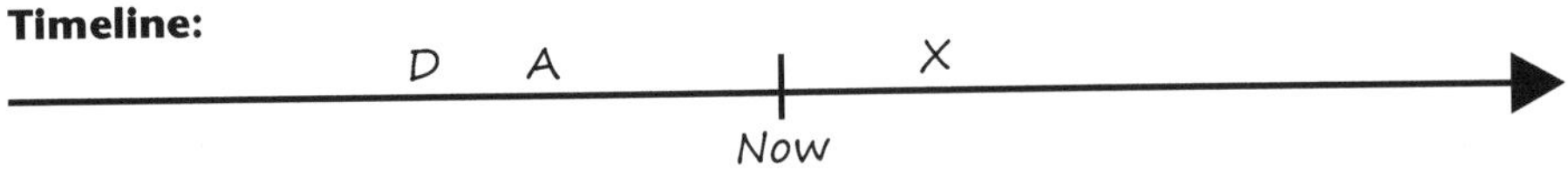

Structure

Positive: subject + be (conjugated) + V-ing
Negative: subject + be (conjugated) + not + V-ing

Examples:

They're running a good campaign.
I'm not taking the English exam this summer.
What are you doing?

Interrogative: [question word] + be (conjugated) + subject + V-ing

Future continuous

When used:

- for things that will happen in the normal course of events, rather than being part of your plans and intentions
- for actions that will be unfinished at a certain time in the future

Timeline:

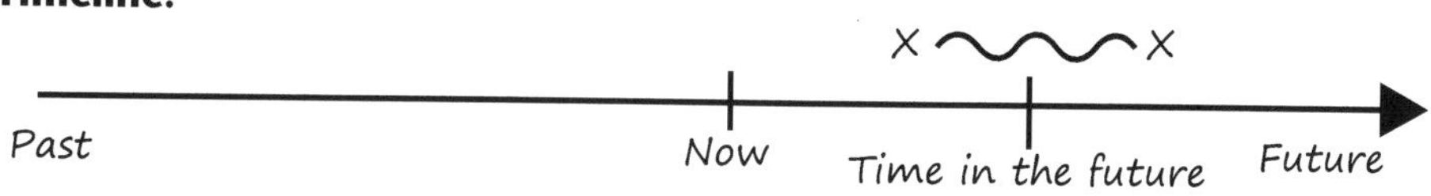

Positive: subject + will be + V-ing
Negative: subject + won't be + V-ing
Interrogative: [question word] + will + subject + be + V-ing

Examples:

This time next year I'll be living in Amsterdam.
I won't be working here after my contract runs out.
What will you be doing in six months' time?

Future perfect simple

When used:

- for actions that will be completed before a specific future time, but the exact time is unimportant
- when making assumptions about actions that are finished now
- often with the phrase 'by the time'

Timeline:

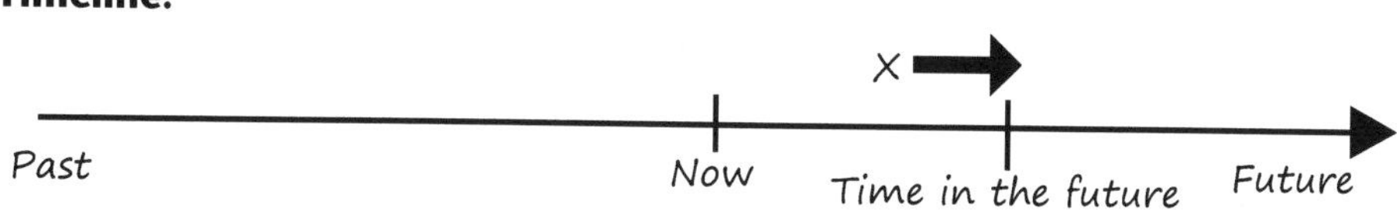

Positive: subject + will have + V3
Negative: subject + won't have + V3
Interrogative: [question word] + will + subject + have + V3

Examples:

By this time next year, I'll have completed my degree.
We can't go to Jane's house; she won't have finished work yet.
Will you have bought a new car by then?

Future perfect continuous

When used:

- for actions that will be unfinished, but have reached a certain stage by a certain time in the future.
- often with the phrase 'by the time'

Timeline:

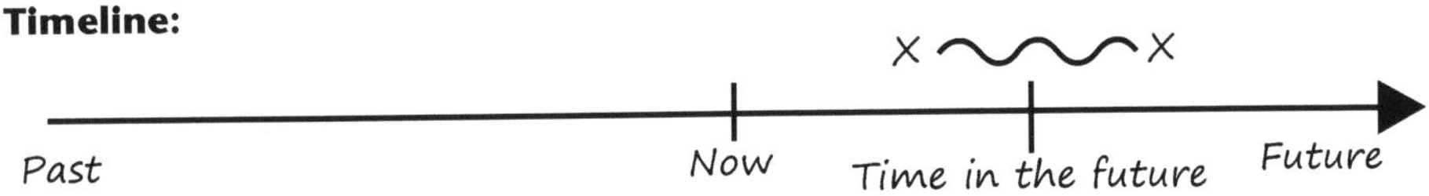

Positive: subject + will have + been + V-ing
Negative: subject + won't have + been + V-ing
Interrogative: [question word] + will + subject + have + been + V-ing

Examples:

By the time I go home, I'll have been working for 17 hours!
Don't expect a guided tour from Alice when we go to Paris next month, she won't have been living there long enough.
How long will you have been studying English for by the time you go home?

Word order in questions

When we ask questions in English the word order is important.
We may not always use all of the columns (depending on the question) but the order of the words is shown in the table below.

Question word	Auxiliary verb	Subject	Main verb	Phrase
	Are	they	coming?	
What	do	you	think	of the new Bond film?
When	is	the game	starting?	
Why	can't	they	be	quiet?
	Have	we	sent	Paul an invitation?
Where	has	Sarah	put	the car keys?
How often	do	the trains	run?	
*Who			won	the race?

*In this example the question word **is** the subject, so we don't use an auxiliary verb or extra subject.

Conditionals

Conditionals are built from two main clauses, the 'if clause (condition)' and the 'main clause (result)', in one of the two orders shown below.

If clause/condition	,	Main clause/result	.

Main clause/result	If clause/condition	.

There are four conditional tenses:

Zero conditional, used for facts.
First conditional, used for possible/real future situations.
Second conditional, used for hypothetical/unlikely future situations.
Third conditional, used for hypothetical past situations.

Zero conditional: we use present simple in both the 'if' and 'main' clauses, e.g.:

If/when you heat water to 100 degrees, it boils.

First conditional: we use present simple in the 'if clause' and future simple in the 'main clause', e.g.:

I'll call you if I find your umbrella.

Second conditional: we use past simple in the 'if clause' and *would/could/might* in the 'main clause', e.g.:

If I won the lottery, I'd travel the world forever.

Third conditional: we use past perfect in the 'if clause' and *would/could/might have* + V3 in the 'main clause', e.g.:

If I had arrived on time, I wouldn't have missed my flight.

Note: we can also **mix** the second and third conditionals if the condition is in the past, but the result is in the present or future, e.g.:

If I had woken up ***earlier, I would be on the plane now****.*

Passives

We use the passive voice when:

- the **object** of the action is more important than the **agent** (person who does the action)
- we don't know who the agent is
- the agent isn't important
- we want to be more objective

To form the passive in any tense, we use the structure:

subject + be (conjugated) + V3

Subject is the object of the action; ***be*** takes the structure of the tense; V3 of the action verb.

Consider: ***Thieves have stolen my car!***

The car is more important than the thieves, so we want to use the passive.

- So, my car becomes the subject of the new sentence [***My car***].
- The sentence is in the present perfect (have +V3) so 'Be' must take that form [***has been***].
- The original verb is steal, so we need to use V3 [***stolen***].

The passive sentence is '***My car has been stolen***' (adding '*by thieves*' is possible, but not necessary).

Common forms of the passive

Subject + passive verb + to-infinitive

They are believed to be hiding in caves in the mountains.

He is thought to be the most famous writer ever.

There + passive verb + to be

There are thought to be approximately 5 million refugees.

There were said to be 75 people on the boat.

It + passive verb + 'that' clause

It is claimed that they entered the country illegally.

It is predicted that global warming will cause many more hurricanes in Europe.

Printed in Great Britain
by Amazon

44701945R00079